Dr Katherine Lack graduated from Somerville College Oxford in 1980. She is a freelance writer and lecturer in church history, with a particular interest in the lessons the medieval period has for us today. The discovery of a pilgrim burial in Worcester Cathedral gave her a window onto the road to Compostela, a road which in the opinion of the sixteenth-century scholar Andrew Borde was 'the greatest jurney that an Englyshman may go'. Katherine Lack is married to an Anglican clergyman and has one son; they live in an Elizabethan cottage in the Welsh Marches. Her previous book, *The Eagle and the Dove*, is a biography of St Columbanus.

For Sally,
interpreter and uncomplaining fellow-pilgrim,
and Paul,
who made it possible

The Cockleshell Pilgrim

A Medieval Journey to Compostela

Katherine Lack

First published in Great Britain in 2003

Society for Promoting Christian Knowledge
36 Causton Street
London SW1P 4ST
www.spckpublishing.co.uk

British Library Cataloguing-in-Publication Data
A catalogue record for this book is available from the British Library

ISBN 978–0–281–05590–6

Typeset by Hardlines Ltd, Charlbury, Oxford
First printed in Great Britain by Bookmarque Ltd, Croydon, Surrey
Subsequent digital printing in Great Britain

Contents

List of Illustrations

Acknowledgements

A unique twentieth-century discovery has opened a door onto the commonplaces of medieval pilgrimage. My first debt of gratitude is to those who made that discovery and made it available, especially Helen Lubin and Philip Barker, the Worcester Cathedral archaeologists at the time, and Charles Kightley who first found Robert Sutton in the city archives; also, to members of the present cathedral staff, in particular David Morrison the librarian, and Chris Guy the archaeologist.

I am also indebted to the Confraternity of Saint James, in London, inheritors of the tradition of care for pilgrims and their practical needs. It has been a privilege to be drawn into their fellowship, and an honour to hold their Patricia Quaife Research Grant for 2000–2 for archive studies. Lack of space restricts me to naming four members who must stand as representatives of all those who have helped me in various ways: Francis Davey, Laurie Dennett, Marion Marples and Patricia Quaife.

The field work in France was greatly helped by my tenure of the Somerville College Edith Haynes Scholarship for 2000–1. Tracing the most likely route for the pilgrimage depended on many factors – early itineraries, trade routes, river crossings and topography, to name but a few. It was remarkable how often the archive materials agreed with surviving evidence on the ground, despite six centuries of change, so there was seldom much doubt which way the pilgrim would have gone. It was sometimes unnerving to feel how closely I identified with him on his journey. The international nature of the Compostela pilgrimage is timeless, and one of its greatest gifts: I hope that everyone who knows they met me on the road will find traces of their contribution in these pages, while being assured that no living individuals can be identified.

Many of the source texts were in languages, medieval and modern, beyond my competence. I am grateful therefore to the band of helpers who came to my rescue, often at short notice; but where no credit is given for a translation, the responsibility is mine. Special thanks are due to Sally Jones, who also nobly drove thousands of miles around western France and across Spain, and to my long-suffering husband Paul, who helped with the English route. To them this book is dedicated.

I would like to thank the following for their particular contributions: the Revd Jackie Davies for help with Latin translations, Mrs Elizabeth Lack and Andrew and Helen Lack for frequent hospitality in Oxford, Cynthia Waterman for her illustrations and timely assistance with Spanish e-mails, M. Julien Deshayes, M. Vincent Juel and Mme Yvetot in Normandy, M. Claude Pain and M. Riquet in Niort, John Clarke at the London Museum, Tim Bridges, Hal Dalwood, James Dinn and other members of the Worcester Archaeology Service, David Calvert, Margaret Goodrich, Dr Barbara Harvey, Dr Pat Hughes, Kathy Lawrence, Janet Maxwell-Stewart, Brian Spencer, Dominique Vaughan-Williams, Martin Wright at Salisbury Museum, and the librarians at the Borda in Dax, Leominster Public Library and the Bodleian Library, Oxford.

Finally, I want to thank Christopher for being so tolerant of his mother while this book has been in gestation.

*

Extracts from the following are reproduced with permission:

The Book of Margery Kempe, edited by S. Meech (1940), reprinted by permission of Oxford University Press.

The Dance of Death by John Lydgate, edited by F. Warren (1931), reprinted by permission of Oxford University Press.

Holinshed's Chronicles, edited by R. S. Wallace (1923), reprinted by permission of Oxford University Press.

The Libelle of Englyshe Polycye, edited by G. Warner (Clarendon 1926), reprinted by permission of Oxford University Press.

The Minor Poems of John Lydgate Part I: Religious Poems, edited by A. K. Donald (1895), reprinted by permission of Oxford University Press.

The Miracles of St James, edited and translated by Thomas F. Coffey, Linda Kay Davidson and Maryjane Dunn. Copyright 1996 by Italica Press, New York. Used by permission.

A Parisian Journal, edited and translated by Janet Shirley (Clarendon 1968), reprinted by permission of Oxford University Press.

William Langland's Piers Plowman, translated by A. V. C. Schmidt for World Classics (1992), reprinted by permission of Oxford University Press.

William Worcestre's Itineraries, edited by John Harvey (Clarendon 1969), reprinted by permission of Oxford University Press.

From Worcester to Compostela

Setting the Scene

This is a reconstruction of one man's attempt to walk from England to Spain, to worship at the shrine of St James at Compostela. A medieval Englishman, with a medieval English point of view.

Ever since word spread that St James's body had been discovered, in a land then dominated by the Moors, the tomb had been a focus for Christian devotion and a rallying point for opposition to Islam. Throughout the Middle Ages, countless pilgrims made their way each year to Compostela, and a complete economic and political framework grew up to control them and to cater for their needs. But it was not a rigid system. Times changed, the needs of pilgrims altered, regional loyalties ebbed and flowed. A few literate travellers left accounts of their journeys, but before the next generation could benefit from them, much would have been out of date. How could ordinary folk plan their pilgrimage?

In 1423, when this account is set, England and France had already been at war for 85 years. Amid unimaginable suffering, France had descended into anarchy and civil war, torn apart by her great magnates. King Charles VI had become insane. His estranged wife had declared that their heir Charles was a bastard. Henry V of England, having already conquered most of northern France, had married the French princess, Katherine, and so become heir to her father's kingdom. Now, with Charles VI and Henry V both dead, the infant Henry VI was nominally King of both nations. But a helpless babe in arms was no substitute for the magnificent Henry V. The 'so-called dauphin' Charles and his Armagnac party still clung on to the loyalty of much of central France, until the war-lords saw which way the wind would blow. In six years, the tables would turn decisively in their favour with the arrival on stage of Joan of Arc. Meanwhile, the war was being fought on a second front in the south-west, where the Armagnacs faced English Gascony and the Anglophile Pyrenean kingdom of Navarre. Beyond the mountains, Castilian Spain was anti-English and sometimes willing to take active steps to help her enemies.

At such a time, what sort of Englishman would consider walking through France and Spain to Compostela? Why would he want to go? Why walk, when so many of his compatriots made the journey by sea, by the boat-load? And if he must go, how would he have managed? What chance did he have of reaching his goal? Where did he sleep, what did he eat, who helped him on his way? What did he think of the places and people he saw?

History in the Middle Ages is often a catalogue of kings, a tale of battles and treaties, of murder and intrigue in high places. For the common people, a broad brush has to serve, or the particular is forced to stand as an example for all. For this one particular man, enough evidence survives to flesh out his bones, to paint his background and his world-view, and to show how his pilgrimage might have been. The framework, in other words, is 'fact', the journey is a 'fiction'.

PART I

The Cockleshell Pilgrim

1

Tomb, Testament and Tower

Can these bones live?[1]

They found his boots first. A day that began with a routine check on the state of the foundations ended in high drama. There, under the tower of Worcester Cathedral, a pair of leather toe-caps met the startled gaze of the excavators. Further investigation revealed the carefully buried remains of a fully clothed man, dressed in loose woollen garments and knee-length boots. Strongly made leather boots, with no heel but thick soles and round comfortable-looking toes. Boots made for walking. The man had once been tall and of robust physique, but he had died crippled with arthritis. Beside him were a staff with an iron tip, a cockleshell, and some fragments of bay and willow leaves. His head and neck were missing.[2]

*

This anonymous burial caused great excitement when it was first discovered. Nothing quite like it had been found before. Who could he have been, to be buried like this? If he had been a priest, he might have been buried with a chalice and paten, the tools of his trade. If he had been a bishop, he should have been in vestments and with his crozier. Laymen were usually buried wrapped only in a shroud, out in a cemetery. To be interred in a cathedral, with such ceremonial as this man appeared to have received, meant he was someone special.

But yet the grave was unmarked, and no record describes his funeral: to the wider world, he was a nobody.

Above all, why bury him in his boots? The Christian life has often been compared with a journey, a pilgrimage to the promised land. But these were not symbolic boots. They had been worn, and they had been cut open to squeeze them on his feet when the body was prepared for burial. They were practical, well made and strong. Boots for going on a journey. The stick, too, was not just a wand of office, but a stout cleft-ash staff, ideal for crossing rough terrain, or fording streams, or warding off angry dogs. Could it be that the boots and staff were there as a deliberate reminder of the man's chief claim to fame, the thing that he most wanted to be remembered for? Seen in this light, the whole burial makes more sense. The man was dressed in the simple woollen habit that was almost a uniform for people travelling on foot to the great medieval shrines, with the special staff that was imbued with mystical significance in medieval minds. He was buried, in fact, as a pilgrim.

But what sort of person might this 'Worcester Pilgrim' have been? When might he have been buried? And why bury him in this way? The location of his grave gives several clues. He was buried beside an internal wall, which formed the back of the monks' choir. This was as hallowed a spot as a layman could normally aspire to, in the concentric system of medieval sanctification. Only those such as King John were desperate enough to buy a resting place within the holy ambience of Worcester's choir itself. This internal wall was built in 1374, as part of a remodelling of the cathedral, and the pilgrim burial must post-date it. But it must have been earlier than the 1540s, when the Reformation outlawed English pilgrimages, because after that no one would have been publicly buried in this way.

Expert analysis of the boots and clothing suggests that the burial is unlikely to be earlier than the mid-fifteenth century. More precise dating is difficult, partly because most systems for dating footwear rely mainly on shoe fashions as shown in medieval art and manuscript illuminations. The boots on this pilgrim are not fashion items, and are of a type rarely represented in art. Long walks and fashionable footwear seldom mix.

So the burial can be dated to somewhere between the mid-fifteenth and early-sixteenth centuries.

The bones of this fifteenth-century man are also quite revealing. They show that he was well fed in childhood, and so presumably belonged to the affluent classes: the frequent shortages and occasional famines of the Middle Ages had left him physically unscathed, whatever their emotional toll. He was a good height for his generation (just over 170cm; 5'7") and well built. But despite his relatively comfortable upbringing, he seems to have been particularly well muscled, especially in his legs and right arm. Even allowing for the more arduous lives of our medieval ancestors, it looks as though he might have undertaken long journeys on foot, over a prolonged period of time, and could well have used a staff grasped in his right hand. This is particularly noticeable because from his middle years he was increasingly affected by arthritis, the signs of which contrast painfully with the evidence of his earlier activity.[3] The skeletal evidence, then, is at least compatible with his having been a 'real' pilgrim.

The best guide to whether a burial is a true 'pilgrim burial' is the presence of badges or tokens, brought back from the shrines visited. Many of these shrines had official tokens: a St Thomas for Canterbury, a scallop shell for Compostela in Spain, crossed keys for Rome, Our Lady for Walsingham, and so on. These could be purchased by the successful pilgrim, from licensed sellers, and were worn thereafter with great pride. At first these tokens were displayed in a variety of places, on the belt, on the knapsack or scrip, or on the clothing. But by the fifteenth century, evidence from statues and stained glass shows that a tradition had arisen of displaying collections of pilgrim badges pinned or sewn on to the distinctive wide-brimmed pilgrim hat. And here, of course, is our problem. For despite his generally good state of preservation, the Worcester Pilgrim is headless, the west end of his grave having been accidentally destroyed in some undocumented Victorian works.

So, while the skeleton and the staff suggest that this is indeed a real pilgrim, the only other evidence left to us seems to be the oddments found in the grave: a pierced cockle shell, and the bay and willow leaves. None of them adds up to much alone, but together they whisper suggestively. Bay has for centuries been equated with laurel, a symbol of great achievement, and the willow might be either for mourning or a substitute for palm, used in the Middle Ages to represent pilgrimage. The cockle shell is more enigmatic still. It looks superficially like a smaller version of the scallop, an ancient and universal symbol of pilgrimage which gradually became equated more specifically with the shrine of St James at Compostela. For centuries this was one of the most important pilgrim destinations of the Christian world. A pilgrim setting off from Worcester might have pierced and worn a local cockle shell as a token of his intention to reach his destination, but whatever the sentimental value of such a shell, once he had reached Compostela an official scallop badge would become proof of his achievement, fixed to his hat for all to see. The cockle might well have been kept, and been interred with him at his request, but it could certainly not be taken as proof of a pilgrimage to St James, then or now.

So here we have a 'Cockleshell Pilgrim'. A fragile story full of tantalizing possibilities. A layman of enough status and wealth to be buried in the cathedral. An unknown man who wished to be remembered as a pilgrim, but whose headless body just fails to yield the necessary clues to his life. He was locally important, respected and presumably pious. Can we find out who he was?

*

The nobility have always been remembered after death. By late medieval times, the middle ranks, too, were not departing without trace: they were making wills. Fortunately for this quest, there are a significant number of surviving examples of Worcester wills from the mid-fifteenth century onwards. Almost all of them make requests concerning the preferred place of burial. Most early-medieval Worcester burials were in the cathedral cemetery, but by the fifteenth century a wider choice of sites was available, and ten of the surviving wills from this period request burial within the cathedral itself. Could one of these possibly be the Pilgrim?

Three of these testaments contain potentially relevant clauses. John Grafton, who made his will in 1484, requested burial before the image of St Christopher, who was the patron and protector of all travellers, however short the journey: most medieval churches had an image of St Christopher, often a wall painting, facing you as you entered the building, but its location in the medieval cathedral is not known and there is nothing in Grafton's will that links him directly with pilgrimage. A more intriguing will is that of Robert Sutton, alias Dyer, which is dated October 1454. He requested burial before the image of St James, a highly suggestive fact since James was the main English patron of pilgrims. A few folios further on in the city collection is another will, that of Robert Sutton's wife Johanne. Dated 7 March 1457, it proves that Sutton was buried in the cathedral, for she simply asks to be buried there beside him.[4] Tantalizingly, it is not known if there is a contemporary female burial beside the Pilgrim.

Could the Worcester Pilgrim really be identified as Robert Sutton? We may never know for certain, but is there more evidence that points towards the possibility? What can be discovered that might connect an anonymous medieval grave to the will of a medieval man with no identified burial site?

Two small general items first. Sutton said in his will that he was of sound mind but sick in body, a standard phrase perhaps, but one that certainly fits with the agony of the Pilgrim's fused and twisted arthritic spine. And he donated a total of £3. 6s. 8d. to the cathedral for his privileged tomb. One pound of this (about two months' wages for a skilled craftsman) was specifically to ensure he obtained a prime site for his burial. So far, tomb and testament agree.

Analysis of the Pilgrim's bones has revealed that he was about sixty years old when he died. This is by no means an extreme age for his generation, but nevertheless unusual: less than half the adult population lived so long. Robert Sutton is very conspicuous for the span of time over which his name continues to appear in the city archives as an adult: a total of 33 years. He was, in fact, a 'survivor' in his generation.

The pilgrim staff, too, yields a further interesting clue. Not only is it apparently a real walking staff, not merely an ornament, but it is coated with a deep-purple paint, probably as a symbol of mourning. This paint seems to be a mixture of bone-black and a far more costly red called kermes, which was made from the bodies of female oak-gall-producing insects. It was used in the exclusive, top-quality end of the medieval dyeing trade, for fabrics such as silks, and was imported from the Mediterranean, especially from Bosnia and Castile.[5] Whereas the cheaper pigments were typically a few pence a pound, even buying Seville kermes grain in bulk from Bristol docks would have cost about 4s. a pound.[6] (Labourers at this time earned 3d. a day, so a pound of kermes would represent three weeks' wages.) Kermes was not normally used as a paint, and other red colours were available much more cheaply: brazilwood and orchel, for example, were both imported up the Severn. So a dyer's business such as the Suttons' was not only one of the few places in Worcester to have ready access to kermes, it was one of only a handful of city households that would have thought to use it in its funeral arrangements.

Robert Sutton, then, died at about the right time and at about the right age to be the Worcester Pilgrim. His interest in St James and his bequests to the cathedral, as well as his work as a dyer, all point to the possibility of these being his remains. It is clear from his wife's will that he was buried in the cathedral. What further evidence is there that might identify him as the Pilgrim?

*

Likewise I bequeath 6 shillings and eight pence to the high Altar of my Parish Church for tithes and oblations forgotten. Likewise to the fabric of my parish church of Saint Andrew, Worcester, ten pounds for the vaulting of the bell tower of the same. Likewise I leave 40 shillings for the paving of the aforesaid church of Saint Andrew.

In the mid-fifteenth century, St Andrew's parish in Worcester was in buoyant mood. Wealthy parishioners like the Suttons, prospering as the cloth trade flourished, were rebuilding their little Norman church. Robert's bequest is particularly generous. After the standard safety clause of 6s. 8d., or half a mark, for any fixed dues he may have overlooked (which technically could be punished with an automatic exclusion from heaven – a sort of medieval red card), he made detailed provision for his contribution to the fabric appeal: £10 for the roof vault of the new tower, and £2 for the church floor.

His widow was less specific; she merely topped up his gift with a further pound.

The tower of the new St Andrew's is a major landmark even in modern Worcester, surmounted as it is by the eighteenth-century 'Glover's Needle', a stone spire that competes with the cathedral for domination of the skyline. But in the Middle Ages it was an even more prominent feature, with a wooden spire only 6 metres lower than the present Needle. The church stood on a rise above the busy quays, and the tower housed a set of bells, the largest of which was used to summon the city council to the nearby Guildhall. To be remembered as a leading donor to its fabric was to be associated for ever with the worship of God and the prosperity of the city. And medieval wills were a sacred trust. It was an absolute obligation to see them executed.

Most of St Andrew's church is gone now, demolished and replaced with a public garden. But the tower remains, and inside it is a magnificent set of fifteenth-century roof bosses. They date to the decade after Sutton's death, and the money he earmarked so carefully in his will would have been just right for the job, including the paint.[7] Most of them are representations of saints, or scenes from the Bible.[8] St Andrew is there, with his saltire cross, and Matthew the tax-collector with a large bag of money, while St Peter holds up a huge key. St James the Great appears not as a martyred Apostle, but in his alternative guise as a Pilgrim, barefoot, staff in hand, scrip slung on a diagonal shoulder strap, and behind his head what seems to be a scallop shell, symbol of the pilgrimage to his principal shrine at Compostela in north-west Spain. This use of a scallop behind the saint's head is highly unusual, suggesting detailed personal instructions to the mason, in order to make the pilgrimage connotations quite clear. The only other place it has been found is on a fifteenth-century Compostelan pilgrim badge.[9]

There is also a 'donor boss' on the vault. These are usually bland stylized representations of husband and wife, holding scrolls on which a prayer would have been painted in Latin. This one is placed between the bosses of St Andrew, the patron of the parish, and St James, which might be a further piece of evidence, except that this James is St James the Less, not James the Great of pilgrimage fame.

Maybe the juxtaposition of donor boss and James is a mere coincidence, or perhaps it is an example of the mistakes that dog the best-laid plans; the result, possibly, of an illiterate workman trying to carry out written instructions? Examples of similar mistakes are known from other church furnishings of this period. The scene on the donor boss, however, has clear implications. The two kneeling figures are presumably Robert and Johanne Sutton. She is a typical representative fifteenth-century gentlewoman, but he, most unusually, has a broad-brimmed pilgrim-type hat slung over his shoulder. He also seems to be wearing a short cape, such as was worn by travellers, thrown onto his back. And is it just imagination, or does careful scrutiny of the hat brim reveal a raised area that might once have been picked out in white or yellow as a scallop? Is this the head and hat of Robert Sutton, his real ones accidentally removed from his grave but marvellously represented here in stone as his memorial?

The choice of imagery in the other bosses also reveals much about the interests of the man who commissioned them. Apart from the Twelve Apostles, there are two scenes from the life of the Virgin Mary, patron of the cathedral where he was buried, and a beautiful representation of the Trinity. The north side has a lively Adoration of

The 'donor boss' from St Andrew's Worcester

the Magi, with a young Balthasar fashionably dressed in a daringly short tunic. The Magi were especially popular in the fifteenth century, venerated as saints and the focus of an international pilgrimage to their supposed tombs at Cologne. Chaucer's legendary Wife of Bath had them on her 'been there' list. The remaining three bosses cannot be identified with complete confidence, but they are probably St Thomas of Canterbury, Edward the Confessor, and either St George or St Michael. All four had major medieval pilgrim cults, focused at Canterbury, Westminster, Windsor and the twin sites of St Michael's Mount and Mont St Michel. All are places where any committed pilgrim might have been.

*

There is one more significant passage in Sutton's long and complex will:

> ... *I also bequeath 20 shillings to the Brothers Minor of Worcester to sing my requiem. Also to the Preaching Brothers of Worcester the same sum of 20 shillings. And for the new cloister of the same house 40 shillings. And also to the fraternity of St James in that same place 20 shillings.*

The Brothers Minor (the Franciscans) did well with Sutton's bequest of 20s, but the Preachers (the Dominicans) certainly did better. Possibly this was simply because they were relatively recent arrivals in Worcester, and were still trying to get their convent built. It was located in the part of the city where the cloth trade was focused, so as a dyer Sutton may also have been drawn naturally into their orbit. But were there more specific reasons?

The Dominican house was the base for the Fraternity of St James, to which Sutton seems to have belonged, despite the fact that his house was in a different part of the city. Unfortunately, nothing else can be said with certainty about this organization, since Sutton's will is the only known reference to it. But it clearly covered a broader geographical area than an ordinary parish-based medieval guild devoted to a patron saint. Dozens of these St James fraternities are known from mainland Europe at this time, and they all seem to relate specifically to the Compostelan pilgrimage. At first, membership was rigidly restricted to those who had successfully completed the journey. Their funerals were then in due course marked with great respect by the other members, including in at least some cases burial with the accoutrements of the pilgrimage. But by Sutton's time, the rich could 'buy into' the spiritual benefits of a connection with St James, leaving money in their wills for men to go to Compostela on their behalf. It is a noteworthy feature of Sutton's will that, with all the money at his disposal, and in spite of his clear interest in St James, he makes no requests for any such vicarious pilgrimages. This strongly suggests he had already been there in person.

So, was Robert Sutton the man now known as the Worcester Pilgrim? If not, the burial must be of another very like him. In a world where the finger of Death pointed and beckoned without warning, he survived to old age and was buried in the cathedral. Devoted to the Virgin and St James, he had a particular fondness for the symbols of pilgrimage, and wished to be clearly remembered that way. He belonged to the city-wide Fraternity of St James. He had, in fact, the means and the motivation.

Suppose we assume that Sutton was buried as the Pilgrim. If so, he must have been born about the year 1390, and would have been nine when Henry IV seized the throne and set up the Lancastrian dynasty. He would have been 15 when Owain Glyndwr marched on Worcester and the King stayed in the city while putting down the rebellion. He would have been 18 in the bitter winter of 1408, when the rivers froze hard, and 25 when the news came of the glorious victory at Agincourt.

What can we reconstruct of Sutton's life in Worcester in the fifteenth century?

Suppose that one spring day he set off on a great undertaking, to make the pilgrimage to St James at Compostela. Why did he do it? Which way would he have gone? What would he have encountered on the way? What chance did he have of completing the journey? Can we begin to understand what motivated him and all the other thousands of pilgrims who daily travelled the roads of medieval Europe? What would it really have been like for a prosperous man like him to take to the road and attempt to walk for six long months for St James?

2

A Medieval Man

You may be someone who speaks the truth and turns an honest penny; you may be as chaste as a baby that cries in church; but unless you really love, and give to the poor a goodly share of the goods that God sends you, you derive no more credit from attending mass and saying the Offices than Ugly Anna from keeping her virginity, when nobody wants to take it!

Good St James has laid it down in his letter: without actions religion is worth absolutely nothing. It's as dead as a doornail without deeds to drive it home![1]

Robert Sutton was not an average medieval man. He was not one of the movers and shakers of his generation, the men (and very occasionally women) who made history. Neither was he one of the tens of thousands of monks, friars and clerks who made up the framework of the medieval Church. Nor was he one of the unnumbered masses of rural poor or one of the urban underclass, to whom history just happened. He belonged instead to a very small group, the educated urban tradesmen who were just beginning to make their mark on European society. Not wealthy enough to rank among the merchant classes, yet he was a freeman of the city, owning property, sitting on the council, treated with respect in his own small pond.

But within his peer group, he was typical. He ran his own business, lived in his own house with his servants and family, was on familiar terms with half the city, and may have travelled as far as Bristol in the course of his work. He was also, tragically, typical in that he outlived all his children. No offspring, siblings, in-laws or even more distant relations are mentioned in either of the Suttons' wills, and it seems clear that he and Johanne died leaving no relatives to inherit their property. In a generation when family ties were all-important, time and again Sutton saw his friends lose their heirs, carried off by plague and insanitary living, in what he believed was the unshakeable judgement of God.

Sutton first appears in the archives in 1421, as a minor official charged with the unenviable task of supervising a tax collection.[2] It is a conspicuous feature of city life at this time that the men who were given this job seldom rose to high office later in life, but in Sutton's case something was different. The following year he witnessed a lease for his rector, letting out part of the manse garden, and then there is a gap of 11 years, after which he reappears several times as bailiff, one of the two most senior members of the city council.[3] During his term of office, he negotiated a deal permitting the priory to run its water pipes along the city ditch, for which privilege the monks were obliged to supply 'a rose rent annually on the Monday after the Feast of Michaelmas [29 September]'.[4] It is to be hoped that the prior's gardener was up to the task!

The centre of Sutton's life, and the framework within which he assimilated the highs and lows of his existence, was his parish church. Its physical bulk, even in its old Norman form, loomed over the large parish and its liturgy shaped the routines of the inhabitants. As well as three services every Sunday, parishioners were expected to attend on all the major feast days of the year: Christmas, the Apostles, the festivals of the Virgin, and the commemorations of the principal events in the life of Christ. No doubt for some people church attendance was as casual as it has always been, even with the threat of hellfire as an inducement. 'Gluttony', a burlesque figure in Langland's *Piers Plowman*, found plenty of fellow-absentees in Betty the Brewer's alehouse when he got sidetracked on his way to morning Mass and stayed there until evensong. And the next character, Sloth, was no better: 'I can't say my 'Our Father' properly as the priest intones it at Mass. I know some ballads about Robin Hood and Randolph, Earl of Chester, but I don't know any about our Lord or our Lady ... And I'd much rather watch a shoemaker's farce in summer, or laugh at a lot of lying scandal about my neighbours, than listen to all that Gospel stuff . . . As for vigils and fast-days, I give all that a miss.'[5] But upright citizens like Sutton did their utmost to go to church regularly. He made an annual confession and then received Communion at Easter, and throughout the year he witnessed the elevation of the Host at every Mass. Thereby, he believed he was incorporated in the saving miracle of the incarnation.

Religious practice informed Sutton's lifestyle. He gave a tithe of his income to the Church. He gave generous alms to the poor and destitute, as a prescribed Work of Mercy. And he fasted regularly: throughout Lent, on the eve of every festival and on Wednesdays, Fridays and Saturdays, the household ate no meat or other rich food. Instead they had fish, bought from the shops concentrated in nearby St Alban's parish, or taken from their own salted, dried or smoked supplies. The simple logic behind this framework for living is summed up in the pardon that Langland's character Truth gives to the eponymous hero Piers Plowman: 'Do well and have well, and God will receive your soul.'[6]

The annual cycle of the seasons, too, was shaped around St Andrew's. After the too-short summer and the great autumn festivals of Michaelmas and All Saints, the approach to Christmas began. The dark fast-time of Advent led up to the Twelve Days of Christmas, culminating in the feast of Twelfth Night. Then at Candlemas, in February, as winter died, the people processed to church with their lights, which were left to burn in honour of the Virgin. In their place, candles blessed at Mass that day were taken home and used to ward off evil through the coming year. Towards the end of Lent, Palm Sunday was celebrated with a solemn procession around the churchyard, with prayers at the Palm Cross. Then came Holy Week, with the terrible Stripping of the Altars on Maundy Thursday and the Creeping to the Cross on Good Friday, when the people crawled barefoot up the church and kissed the purple-shrouded crucifix. The parishioners clubbed together to pay for food and candles for a watch to be kept over the cross and sacrament, buried in its sepulchre by the high altar until Easter morning. Then it was triumphantly 'raised' and carried round the church, preceded by a great processional cross and accompanied by candles and ringing bells.

Sutton's Worcester was a boom town. The city's location on the River Severn, at one of the lowest bridging points and near the head of the tidal waters, gave it a unique trading position. Three regular weekly markets were supplemented by major annual fairs, when the lowlands to the east traded with the pastoral lands of the west. For nine days around Palm Sunday, the weekend after Easter, and four days each for the Feast of the Assumption (mid-August) and the Nativity of the Blessed Virgin (mid-September), the already bustling city was filled to bursting. The Easter fair, in particular, was famous for its sales of horses and thousands of sheep, brought in from miles around by the lure of regional trade. The Church bore its part in encouraging these events, for they coincided with peak pilgrimage seasons to the cathedral shrines, and represented increased prosperity for all.

In Sutton's time, the single commodity that underpinned the wealth of the city was cloth. Less raw wool was now being exported, and England was producing increasing quantities of high-quality cloth herself. Worcester was unusual in that just north of the city were convenient streams where the necessary fulling mills could be built. So while other old wool centres decayed, Worcester did well, and Sutton was able to take advantage of it. Wool was brought into the city by river and road, then spun, woven and barged upstream using the last of the tidal benefit. After fulling it was sent down again to the northern quays. Then after further treatment some was shipped out as white cloth, while the rest was dyed for home consumption and the fine export trade. By the fifteenth century, the city had grown to be among the 15 most prosperous in the land, with a population of about 3,000.

The important men, the backbone of the city, lived in smart houses in and around the High Street, and in the suburb of St John's to the west. Sutton himself lived on the top side of Huxterestrete (now Copenhagen Street), running down from the High Street to the quays. It was one of the better properties in town, and a century after his death was still remembered as having once been his, in a document 'whereby John Bartenale [sells] a tenement with appurtenances in the city of Worcester in the street called Bradport, adjoining a tenement late belonging to the monastery of St Mary the Virgin of Worcester on the south and the tenement of Thomas Lytulton on the north, and extending from the said street in front to the garden formerly of Robert Sutton, dyer, and which said tenement descended to the donor from his grandfather Nicholas ...'[7] Despite rebuilding and road widening in the last 100 years, the ancient plot boundaries can still be located, fossilized in a Victorian survey of the city.[8] The site of Robert Sutton's old house can clearly be distinguished, its garden abutting at right angles onto the back of the first big property on old Bradport Street.

This upper half of Huxterestrete was lined with large houses, occupied by the richer men of the parish. It had once been part of the affluent Jewish quarter, and it was still paved with careful gold. The frontages were wide, mostly two full 'Worcester' rods (a total of about 10 metres). Behind the imposing half-timbered house, with hall and private chambers, there was an array of outbuildings: a kitchen, a stable, perhaps a pigsty and a chicken coop, a latrine, maybe a bakehouse. Beyond was the garden, supplying the household with medicinal herbs, vegetables like leeks, cabbages and onions, and a range of pot herbs for soups and stews: parsley, pimpernel, groundsel, spinach and fat hen. A constant concern was fire: not only the risk of it, but the supply and storage of fuel. A household this size needed several tons of wood a year, just for the cooking. The dyer's business may have included a workshop and store at the house, but the dyeing itself, with the vats and fires and smells, would be done at a separate site, down by the river. On Eport Street, near the Severn Bridge and the northern quays, there was a long tradition of dyeing and it is there that Sutton's contemporaries in the trade, John Mer, William Mere, William Newemon and Richard Pacey, were based.

City life was tightly controlled, with regulations for everything from licensed premises to road repairs. Prices for basic foodstuffs were set, trading hours were fixed, and strangers staying too long in the city were to be reported to the authorities. Worcester was ruled by two bailiffs and a council of 24, with a greater council of 48. This oligarchy renewed its membership from among a close but fluid group of burgesses, free men of standing and authority in the community. The bailiffs were reimbursed for some of their expenses of office out of statutory fines for breaches of the ordinances, and they rarely served more than two terms. The council made the regulations, enforced them to the best of their ability, and prosecuted offenders. Their chief preoccupation, apart from breaches of the peace and fraudulent trading, was the growing problem of sanitation. The situation was not yet impossible, with many plots still vacant and a good number of private wells. But the tenements had privies in their back gardens, with no regular system for emptying them, and the various workshops added to the contamination, with effluent from slaughterhouses, brewers, dyers, bell-founders and fishmongers seeping into the groundwater or directly into the river. There was a general awareness that foul smells bred disease, and the mess in the streets was often so bad that it was necessary to wear thick-soled wooden pattens to get about, but attempts to control it were still rudimentary:

> *Also, that every man kepe his soyle clene agenst his tenement, and his pavyment hole, in peyne of 40d., half to be payde to the Bayllies, and the other half to the comyn tresor (Ordinance 20) …*

> *Also, that no sadeler, bocher, baker ne glover ne none other persone, caste non intrelle ne fylthe of Bestes donge, ne doust, over Severne brugge, ne beyond the seid Brugge in the streme … in peyne of lesynge 6s. 8d. (Ordinance 51) …*

> *Also, that non persone caste eny donge of eny manere harlotre in the Slippe goynge to Severne at the lode [ford], ner uppon the keye, on peyne of lesynge of 40d. … Also that no maner person withyn the seid cite, have ne suffre non swyne goynge at large, in anoysaunce or grevaunce of hur neyghburgh or eny citezen of the same; (Ordinance 56).*[9]

The medieval city was a tightly knit community, where privacy was unknown. In the interests of communal survival, prying into your neighbour's affairs was meritorious. Conjugal rights, conjugal fidelity, observance of fasts and city ordinances, all these were everybody's concern, lest wrath descend on everyone's head. The worst sins were those that harmed your neighbour most directly: anger, greed, gossip and pride. Life was lived in the public eye, and under the aegis of the saints: a cloud of witnesses as ever-present and vigilant as your earthly neighbours.

Just like your neighbours, the saints watched over your most trivial chores and heard your every vow. For every event there was a patron: St Christopher for travellers, Osmund of Salisbury for the toothache, St Antony of Padua when things were lost. Lovers looked naturally to St Valentine to smooth their path, and unhappily married women could seek help from St Wilgefortis, popularly known as St Uncumber, who had escaped an importunate suitor by miraculously growing a full beard. Name-saints had a particular role, as an extra godparent: St Robert of Knaresborough was a popular English hermit-saint, and the holy oil that oozed from his tomb made it an important pilgrim destination. Such oil, or a cloth that had touched it, could be brought back home and used to treat illness or kept as a memento of prayers answered.

The saints offered many benefits. Their lives and sufferings, recounted in sermons and wall-paintings and in books such as the best-selling *Golden Legend*, were examples of piety and fortitude that were an enduring inspiration. By venerating them, God was honoured and the worshipper strengthened. Communion with them cemented the bonds of spiritual neighbourliness. They were helpers in time of need, and interceded before God for the faithful. Accessible everywhere, the saints were most approachable where they were physically manifest, in statues or relics or wells, and there the devotee was most assured of help. Prayers were answered, and vows could be fulfilled.

Much devotion was lavished on Our Lady of Worcester, a statue of the Virgin in pride of place in the late medieval cathedral. Throughout Sutton's lifetime and up to the Reformation, she stood in her own chapel, probably in the nave and adjacent to the newly extended choir, not far from where the Pilgrim's grave was later to be discovered. People flocked to make her offerings in candles and coin, at all six Marian feasts in the year.[10] In return, they asked her to intervene for them and their loved ones at the Judgement, and they took comfort from her Joys and Sorrows. The roots of this popular synergism are not hard to trace: a mother destined to mourn her only son was, after all, a potent contemporary theme.

Worcester also had other, older, objects of piety. Chief among them were the shrines of the two Saxon bishop-saints, Oswald and Wulstan, up by the High Altar in the choir. Their head-relics were encased in silver and gilt reliquaries, which were displayed to the faithful for a fee. Oswald continued to be useful to the city, for his meteorological abilities. In 1390 there was a great procession involving 44 pounds of wax candles to accompany his relics, to pray for the ending of a drought.[11] In 1437, by contrast, they were carried out by a slightly sceptical but presumably desperate cathedral staff, 'As we byn enformed that hyt hath byn afore this time for cessyng of such continual reyne.'[12]

Among the other treasures of the cathedral were a mitre that Oswald had worn, an arm bone of St Edmund, a silver-mounted arm-relic of St Roman the Bishop, a small relic of St Margaret, and many clothes and ornaments of Wulstan, Oswald, Dunstan, Alphege and other holy men and women. But it was Our Lady of Worcester that was drawing the crowds. Offerings at the main cathedral shrines had dwindled away and were only a fraction of those collected in her new chapel.[13]

When trouble came to Robert Sutton's generation, they pleaded with their patron saint. Or they bent a penny in honour of a miracle worker who had helped their friends, making it commercially valueless but spiritually potent. They vowed to visit a particular shrine if they were granted a favourable outcome, or undertook pilgrimages prescribed in penance for sin. So it was that candles were lit on parish altars in gratitude, and regional saints like Thomas of Hereford continued to draw local people long after their brief blaze of national prominence was over: he was their saint and he took care of his own. Thus it was also that some shrines developed a life of their own, because once made, the vow had been accepted in heaven and must be fulfilled. Rome, Jerusalem, Canterbury, Cologne and Santiago de Compostela; these were some of the places people vowed to visit in time of terror. In storms, disease, bereavement and disaster, the promise of a pilgrimage was the best way to reach the ears of the saints. The undertaking might be personal or vicarious, but if solemnly vowed and rightly carried out, the heavenly bargain would be kept.

PART II

England

3

On the Road

'By St James', swore the knight, 'I solemnly agree to do just what you say for every day I live upon this earth!'
'I, for my part', replied Piers, 'will dress myself in pilgrim's clothes and travel with you until we find Truth.'[1]

What might have driven a man like Robert Sutton to set off on a major pilgrimage? There were local shrines in plenty where he could go for his normal needs. His arthritis was progressive and already painful, but he need not have gone far for that. St Winefrede's curative water at Holywell was less than a week away. And the pope had declared a special decade of indulgence at Hailes Abbey in the Cotswolds from February 1413, during which the phial of Holy Blood was displayed at Whitsun and Corpus Christi. A pilgrimage there, combined with a donation for the repair of the abbey, guaranteed a fixed remission of penance, and might have eased his aching bones. It took something bigger to wrench a man from his accustomed piety and impel him to risk his life on such a journey to the edge of the world.

Sutton was driven, above all, by the inexorable, mathematical logic of his belief system. The wages of sin is death. Confession and absolution with performance of penance, as prescribed by Mother Church, counterbalanced sin. For an orthodox believer like him, personal disaster meant there had been personal sin. The greater the disaster, the greater the sin must have been, and therefore the greater the penance required.

In the hot summer of 1422, children and grown men died like flies in the cities of Europe. In the English siege camp before Meaux in France, King Henry sickened and finally succumbed to a mysterious illness, brought on, it was thought, by his plans to move the relics of a jealous local saint. In Paris, 'more children had smallpox this year, because of the extreme heat, than anyone had ever known before, and they were so covered with it as to be unrecognisable ... Certainly very many small children were extremely ill with it and either died of it or were left blinded'.[2] Such visitations were a sure sign of divine displeasure.

In Worcester that summer it was also hot, and the stage was set for a tragedy to unfold. How natural it would have been for Sutton, in the confines of a crowded and sweltering city, to find himself distracted by the attentions of another woman, while Johanne was occupied at home. Low-cut bodice, trim waist, a friendly voice, smiling eyes. Too hot to be always supervising the work at the dyers vats; too much time idling, dreaming, imagining. But 'natural' for his generation did not mean 'acceptable'. Quite the reverse, it meant fallen, sinful, unredeemed. Sutton would certainly remember it when the bloody flux came to the city, killing some and weakening many others, including his own family.[3] And he would be tormented by the memory of it when the smallpox struck, carrying off his child in one anguished week. This was the act of God: inevitable, irrevocable and inscrutable. The wages of sin is death.

For a man of Sutton's religious convictions, the cause and effect would be all too clear, and Father Greene[4] could confirm it when he went in anguish of soul to make his confession: 'whosoever looketh on a woman to lust after her hath committed adultery with her already in his heart';[5] and 'the fathers have eaten sour grapes, and the children's teeth are set on edge'.[6] His sin had been noted and weighed in the balance; such sins, however secret, had consequences that could not be concealed. Bereaved, heartbroken, ashamed and utterly forlorn, Sutton knew he must do penance for his sin, for the child's soul and for his own. Such a scenario, such a reaction and conclusion, is perfectly in keeping with the tenor of the times. Any devout and passionate man would feel the full weight of guilt on his own conscience, and would seek help in addressing it.

Fortunately for him, that help was at hand: a painful but well-ordered path to restoration through suffering and sacrifice. Confession and pilgrimage offered a sure route to forgiveness and restitution, time for meditation and amendment, and the assurance that if he reached his goal he would be absolved, and if he returned home alive he would be redeemed in the eyes of his community. It provided all the ingredients for a cure, through the work of Christ the Healer: the removal of temptation, the sweat of contrition, a curative diet of fasting and penance, the poultice of prayer, and the bloodletting of almsgiving.

Once the diagnosis was made, the prescription followed: pilgrimage overland to Compostela and back, praying at all the major shrines he found on the way, with especial care for those of Our Lady, who interceded for sinners and who knew the pains of the cruelly bereaved. Those who wished to visit the shrine of St James could now do so by boat from Bristol, in a month with good luck and fair weather. Overland, as a penitential exercise, it would take half a year or more. The season was late now, but next year, 1423, was a Holy Year, with the Feast of St James falling on a Sunday, and the promise of plenary indulgence for all who reached the shrine. By setting off just after Easter, Sutton had a good chance of arriving at Compostela in time for St James's Day in July, and returning over the worst of the mountains before the winter snows began.

Once the penance was undertaken, many things had to be arranged before he could set off. Returning pilgrims coming through Worcester spoke of Bristol as the best place to find a boat: '& other pilgrymes that wer at Bristowe, desiryng to spedyn her jurne, went a-bowte fro port to port & sped nevyr the mor. & so thei cam a-geyn to Bristowe, whyl sche lay stille & sped bettyr than they for al her labowr.'[7] To Bristol, then, he would direct his footsteps and see what emerged thereafter.

Meanwhile, he needed to assemble his documentation. A formal consent from Johanne allowed him to undertake the pilgrimage, and a letter of authentication from Rector Greene was required, to set him apart from opportunist wayfarers and beggars and to validate his journey. A safe-conduct in the name of the King would be needed too, but that would be obtained at his port of embarkation. Bills of exchange, made out by the Italian bankers who had begun coming to the great fairs, were a useful means of circumventing the bullion restrictions. They might also provide valuable introductions and certainly lessened the dangers of theft.

At last, after a long dark winter and a more than usually penitential Lent, a cold April blew in and Easter came round. Sutton made his will, to come into effect if he was absent for more than a year and a day, painfully aware as he did so that this pilgrimage was for him a type of spiritual death, even if he survived it physically. At the service of dedication at St Andrew's, the similarity was even more forcibly expressed, as he was confessed and given the consecrated Host as if this were indeed the last rites. He publicly laid his bag and staff on the altar for the blessing: the small pouch that represented the humility he so painfully felt, and the staff for empowerment and the conquest of evil, which he so desperately craved.

Then, with a carefully folded letter from the rector declaring that he had fully confessed and could therefore benefit from absolution at Compostela were he to achieve his goal, or else give him the assurance that he would die fully shriven on the way, he set off to walk through the city with the English words from the service churning through his head:

The Lord uphold thy goings in His paths
That thy footsteps slip not ...

Grant unto Thy servants here present, who are setting forth
from amongst us, the company of guardian angels, that they,
being protected by Thy aid, may be seized by no fear of evil, nor
be smitten by any grievous sickness, nor be troubled by any
enemy lying in wait to assail them ...[8]

He did not walk alone, but in his heart it was the loneliest moment of his life. His fellow citizens gathered to see him on his way, as the rules for a contemporary guild make clear: 'If any brother or sister wishes to make pilgrimage to Rome, St James of Galicia or the Holy Land, he shall forewarn the gild; and all the brethren and sisters shall go with him to the city gate, and each shall give him a half penny at least'.[9] Another guild required that departing pilgrims should be accompanied beyond the city walls, and if news could be obtained, the members should gather there to greet them on their return.

From St Andrew's, the solemn little crowd with Sutton in its midst walked past the Guildhall, on the same site then as its modern successor, and past the cross that dominated the High Street. Down below the cathedral, they left the city by the twin towers of the red stone Sidbury Gate,[10] where the Commandery Hospital cared for its pensioners. Further on in the London Road suburbs, another cross at the foot of Green Hill marked the start of Tewkesbury Lane. And there his companions saw him off on his long pilgrimage. He had not trained for the journey, and he had no detailed itinerary, but he could safely assume that every turn of his road would be marked with a cross. It was, in truth, a journey of faith.

Every stage of that first day's walk remained for ever etched in his mind. He had travelled this road before, several times, but mounted, as a solidly affluent citizen. Now he was on foot, conspicuously dressed and making such slow progress that at times the view hardly changed from one hour to the next. From his strong boots to his three-quarter-length tunic, his cape and his broad-brimmed hat, his clothes were both a distinctive uniform and a highly practical outfit for the job in hand. At the first shower of rain, which was not long in coming, his hat proved its worth, as did his nearly waterproof cape, shedding most of the water that dripped onto his shoulders. But in a society where dress codes for the different social classes were prescribed by law, and where penalties could be imposed for wearing clothes unsuited to one's station in life, he felt the heavy symbolism of setting off in garments more appropriate for a peasant or unskilled labourer. Then, much more than now, a pilgrimage was a social leveller.

And on his previous journeys he had taken a saddle bag for his possessions. Now instead he carried only a scrip, that most characteristic item of pilgrim gear, a small satchel slung crosswise over one shoulder on a long strap. Sutton was accustomed to his creature comforts, but apart from his documents, a bowl and spoon, and a bag of small coin, he carried one change of linen underwear, and nothing more. The significance of this was clearly spelled out in the traditions of the pilgrimage:

> ... *we give them the blessed purse ... [which] signifies the generosity of alms and the mortification of the flesh. A purse is a narrow little bag, made from the hide of a dead animal, with its mouth always open and not bound with ties. That the purse is a narrow sack signifies that the pilgrim, trusting in the Lord, must carry along with him a small and moderate provision. That it is made from the skin of a dead animal signifies that the pilgrim himself must mortify his flesh with its vice and concupiscence, through hunger and thirst, through many fasts, through cold and nakedness, and through many insults and hardships. That it is not bound with ties but that the mouth is always open signifies that one must expend one's own things on the needy, and consequently one must be prepared for receiving and prepared for giving.*[11]

Some of this might be taken with a pinch of salt at first, but it is a symbolism that has stood the test of time. And, once on the road, the truth behind the rhetoric would soon make itself felt. No soap, no soft dry shoes for the evenings, nor any nightwear; no comb, no fur-lined clothes for cold days or cool linens and fine light woollens for the heat, and a vow to add to his normal regime of fasting by eating only the simplest of food, accepting whatever he was offered in charity.

So as he set off, on Easter Monday, 5 April 1423, Robert Sutton was beginning a journey of faith in more ways than one. He travelled as a pilgrim, having shed his familiar position in the city hierarchy. Instead of his money and rank, his pilgrimage had become his key to society. He quickly discovered he had exchanged respect for his wealth for respect for his calling. Complete strangers called out that they would pray for him, knowing that they would thereby share in the merits of his pilgrimage. He travelled with many spiritual certainties, fears as well as comforts, but he had no maps, nor any signposts, and relied entirely on word of mouth. In what condition was the road ahead? Just how long would it take to walk the five leagues to Tewkesbury, his goal for this first day?[12] With few exceptions, long-distance journeys were only the sum of a series of local roads, serving local needs, and his best information was drawn from many pieces of imperfect advice. Sutton's road, therefore, was set in a different psychological landscape to ours, and based on different data, and consequently might follow a different route.

Once his well-wishers had turned back to the city, Sutton set his face to the south. Muddy and ill-defined, the track ran past a couple of poor cottages and then into open fields between Green Hill on his left and the Diglis marshes by the river. Such familiar sights, now seen as if for the first time, as steps towards Compostela. The little Duck Brook was his first hurdle, ten minutes down the lane; a small but significant barrier then, but completely unnoticed by modern travellers. Then he gained a little height and the panorama of the Malvern Hills unfolded. The landscape was largely open: the ancient Forest of Horewell that had once stretched almost down to Tewkesbury had mostly been cleared long before, giving clear views across to the peaks that marched so slowly past him.

One might suppose this route down to Bristol would have been easy to follow, with all the traffic that used the Severn valley. A major Roman road once ran the length of the Welsh borders, passing through Worcester on the way, but by the later Middle Ages it had been largely lost. The first attempt at a detailed survey of England, by John Ogilby in the 1600s, describes it as 'Affording in general no very good road.'[13] A combination of annual flooding, lack of upkeep and deliberate robbing of the stones had led to a general abandonment of the old line, and neither court cases nor the many pious bequests for particular sections had much effect. The river, after all, was a much easier way to carry heavy loads, simpler to regulate and easier to maintain.

At Kempsey, the first village down the road, the 'Old Road South' swung towards the church, in search of a safe place to cross the brook. The road here was so bad that from 1427 to 1448 indulgences were offered to those who contributed to its repair. An example of tidy medieval thinking, this: time off Purgatory for alleviating the pains of the road. Near the imposing church Sutton came to a wide and shallow ford, marked by another cross.[14] Even a much-frequented ford like this, carrying regular wheeled traffic, could cause problems for those on foot. Sutton's walking boots might well have been top of the range, with the new technology of double soles and full turn-welt construction, the second line of stitching giving much greater water resistance. They could comfortably cope with some mud and even a brief encounter with a shallow puddle, and so he might have belonged to the first generation of pilgrims who could hope to spend a good part of their time dry-shod. But nevertheless they were far from waterproof. At a big ford like the one at Kempsey, if the adjacent footbridge was unsafe (as they so often were), he had to take off his boots and paddle. Finding a reliable bridge, or a place where a stream could be jumped, would always be a bonus.

Down to Severn Stoke, the road ran somehow across flat land, by the riverside meadows. Flooded through the winter, and still wet in spring, this land was prime summer grazing and haymaking land, and so it was kept clear of trees. Before long the boots were thoroughly soaked. Severn Stoke itself was a sizeable place, with an old church perilously close to the flood line, and several inns. It even had a market under royal charter, granted in its heyday just before the Great Pestilence came. Today, time, plagues and the changing course of the meandering river have conspired against Severn Stoke, shrinking the village and making the church and the surviving inn more liable to flooding than before. But as the midway point between Worcester and Tewkesbury, it once had an importance all its own, until the turnpike road changed the country for ever.

The pilgrim staff came into its own on the first low hill, horribly slippery at the beginning of a cold damp spring. Across its clay-caked slopes a whole fan of tracks had evolved, each seeking an easier route than the others, and a stout stick was an advantage. And in an age when all men normally went armed, that was not its only use. Despite the law that undergrowth and ditches had to be removed for a full 200 feet (60 metres) either side of the roads, highway robbery and ambush were all too common. Public disorder had contributed to the downfall of King Richard II, and his successors, the Lancastrians, had made strenuous efforts to improve the situation. In theory at least, Sutton would be respected as a pilgrim and be safe from such attacks, but a stout staff taller than himself, with a good knob on the end, was a great comfort, especially to one so recently deprived of his accustomed dagger.

At Holly Green, Sutton's route crossed a much bigger road, the high road from Wales. It came over the Upton ferry, where the river crossing was marked by the church tower, and so into the Avon valley and central England. This road was wide, wide enough for a flock of Welsh sheep or a drove of cattle to pass along it on their journey east, and although rutted and muddy, it was so broad that it was possible to pick a way across it avoiding most of the filth.

Now there was only one more village to go before the end of the day. Over the flood plain of the Severn, with the Malverns still accompanying him to the right, he came down into Ripple along the remnants of the old Roman causeway road.[15] Ripple was an important place, with an impressive cross marking the middle of the settlement. The misericord seats in the church, brand new when Sutton passed this way, show the labours of the months in a thriving agricultural community. By April, spring sowing was mostly over, and the chief concern was to scare the birds off the autumn sowings and the emerging crops.

From Ripple, the road contoured around to the west, keeping just above the winter flood levels. And so Sutton came to the beginning of King John's Bridge, a remarkable construction a bow-shot long, a mixture of high causeway and two bridges that gave access to Tewkesbury on the far bank of the Avon. A remarkable and most admirable piece of public engineering, but even here John's reputation still haunted him:

> King John, who by right of his wife was Earl of Gloucester, caused Tewkesbury Bridge to be built of stone. The person entrusted to carry out this order first made a stone bridge across the main stream of both arms of the river, north and west; but then to save time and money he built a wooden bridge of great length at the northern end across land prone to sudden inundations.[16]

The bridge at the Tewkesbury end is still substantially the medieval one, but the northern bridge and the causeway have, not surprisingly, been repeatedly repaired and rebuilt. In 1367 there was a particularly vitriolic court case over its state of extreme decay, despite the town having been granted a steady income for its maintenance from market-day tolls. In spring 1423, by good fortune, it was in good repair for Sutton's journey.

Tewkesbury has grown greatly since Robert Sutton's day, but the town he walked into, weary and limping a little, but satisfied after his first day on the road, is still essentially the same shape: 'three streets, which meet at the market cross.'[17] Even the bridges still struggle to bear the unsuitable loads forced upon them. Just over the bridge, an inn under the sign of the 'Bear and Ragged Staff' (the Beauchamp family emblem) offered hospitality. A new stable block was built on in 1422, hinting at an increase in trade in newly prosperous times. But for a pilgrim, more suitable accommodation was available at the Benedictine abbey in the centre of the town. There the same restoration of confidence is revealed in a speculative building project of a row of tenements for rent, which still dominates the main street, backing on to the enclosure wall. Although it was not an abbey with any particular claims on a pilgrim, it was pleased to welcome one for a night. It had, moreover, a proud tradition of support for the Beauchamp family and the Lancastrian kings, and was flourishing, self-assured and wealthy.

Here, Sutton was made welcome from the moment he reached the porter's lodge. Travellers, especially the nobility, might be beginning to test monastic generosity, but a genuine pilgrim was a different matter. St Benedict had laid great stress on the obligations of Christian hospitality, and his monks still honoured his injunction to care for the guests, especially pilgrims, 'who are never wanting in a monastery'. In the guest hall at Tewkesbury Abbey that night, Sutton and his fellow travellers found food and comfortable beds, without charge. A clean mattress and linen sheets, candles and some marsh mallow poultice for his heel where one wet boot had rubbed it raw, were all freely given.[18] Then, in the morning, he attended Mass in the abbey nave beneath the soaring new stone vault, and gave a free-will offering from his scrip, for the care of future guests: a first tentative lesson in 'receiving and giving'.

4

By Severn to Bristol

... no sooner has this flow of the sea begun than all the ships at the Hollow Backs, from Spain, Portugal, Bordeaux, Bayonne, Gascony, Acquitaine, Brittany, Iceland, Ireland, Wales and other parts weigh their anchors and set sail for Bristol.[1]

The rest of the overland route to Bristol was much harder going. It was 'a fowle contrye, all in lanes and stonny wayes, betwyxt woodes, without any good refresshynge . . . so evell lanes, and depe dykes, so many hedges, trees, and busshes.'[2]

Beyond the wet ground just south of Tewkesbury, the road climbed a gentle hill and gave a brief but splendid view back to the abbey. Then down to Deerhurst, once a flourishing priory of a French abbey, which had become a hostage to the fortunes of war and been milked of its wealth by the crown, until it was shrunk to a small cell of Tewkesbury Abbey. Its buildings were derelict, its life moved on. For a while, Sutton's road then kept close to the river, but beyond Apperley and its duckpond it began a tortuous hill-hopping route to Gloucester. Bridge maintenance was critical in this landscape interspersed with full streams feeling their way into the Severn. In bad years travel could be impossible for weeks at a time. In 1378, court records show that the Wainlode Bridge across the marshy Chelt valley was broken, and the alternative route via 'Nortonbrigge' a little farther upstream had been 'broken for three years past', despite being the clear and exclusive responsibility of the prior of St Oswald's of Gloucester. In the same year, the road at Deerhurst was ruinous, and that bridge was also broken; the prior of Deerhurst had pleaded in his defence that his little bridge was only supposed to be a footbridge, and it had been destroyed by inappropriate heavy traffic.[3]

Gloucester housed the first important shrine on Sutton's pilgrimage, his goal for the second day. King Edward II had not been a model king, especially when compared with the much lamented Henry V, and his blatant preference for male favourites and their bad advice had been notorious. But he was the Lord's Anointed, and the manner of his deposition and subsequent brutal murder at Berkeley Castle in 1327 was for a long time the subject of horrified popular talk. Thomas Lord Berkeley had rebuilt the parish church at Cam in expiation of his part in the murder, and miracles were soon being reported at Edward's tomb at Gloucester Abbey. Encouraged in part by his son, the new king, who wished to distance himself from his mother and the other plotters of the coup, and in part by the abbey authorities, a cult took shape. If people were healed at the shrine, or believed that the murdered king had helped them when they appealed to him, how could word fail to spread that here was a new saint active in Gloucestershire? The town, once an important river port and trading centre, had been feeling the competition from Bristol farther downstream, so perhaps the new prosperity that 'Saint' Edward brought with him helped to silence any sceptics that remained. St Peter's Abbey[4] was the chief beneficiary, the great upsurge in donations from the faithful enabling the remodelling of the transepts, the modernizing of the choir and the nave exterior, and the construction of a new east window. By 1423, the work was nearly complete, and the abbey presented a beautiful new exterior with clean, sharp lines in the most up-to-date style.

Sutton entered the town through an outer gate with a drawbridge, where six roads met at a cross, and came down Hare Lane to the main north gate through the walls. Skirting the abbey enclosure, he passed through the cordwainers' district with its shoemakers and rich smells of leather, before turning right at the High Cross into Westgate Street. Further along, by the noise and stench of the butchers' quarter, the road narrowed to a jostling bottleneck as it passed the 'King's Board'.[5] Finally, he turned in to the relative calm of the abbey precincts through the diminutive Michaelgate that gave onto the lay cemetery.

Within the abbey church, an ambulatory allowed pilgrims access to the tomb of King Edward without encroaching on the sacred space of the monks' choir. At peak times, the flow of visitors could be regulated with a one-way system to prevent unseemly confusion, and their offerings could be more efficiently collected. The effigy of the King, serene in alabaster on a Purbeck marble tomb, has the face of a sensitive man at rest from a tormented life. At his head and feet, large niches were carved out of the old Norman piers to allow suppliants closer to the sanctified dust. On the high altar, a perpetual light burned for his soul.

In the days before King Edward drew pilgrims in droves, passing travellers could stay at a variety of religious houses in Gloucester. St Bartholomew's Hospital, down by the Westgate Bridge over the Severn, was by far the largest, with a staff of 12 plus ancillary workers, and beds for 90. St Peter's Abbey, St Oswald's Priory with its venerable but unfashionable relics of King Oswald, and the once-wealthy Llanthony Secunda Priory, all welcomed guests, as did the other Orders in the town. But by the time of Sutton's pilgrimage much had changed. The hospitals were caring more for the sick and destitute, and beginning to prefer local paupers to passers-by. St Oswald's and Llanthony were both in straitened circumstances, and the abbey, while eager to encourage the stream of pious visitors that had already lasted nearly a century, could not absorb the numbers without destroying its cloistered calm. So a series of abbey properties in the town were adapted for pilgrim accommodation; with minimal strain the monastery increased its visitor through-put while keeping control of their movements and a large part of their spending.

Three of the earliest of these innovative 'Great Inns' were at the Ram, the Fleece in Westgate, and the New Inn. This last was rebuilt in its present form from 1430, on a grand scale, with massive oak and chestnut beams. Its two courtyards, galleried upper floors capable of sleeping 200 and its large stable block are an impressive testimony to the flourishing pilgrim economy and buoyant spirit of Gloucester in these years. Here there was no infirmarian to treat their sore feet, but for a penny a night the pilgrims slept in comfort and relative security, three to a wide bed, between clean sheets and with fresh rushes and aromatic herbs strewn on the floor. For another penny, the landlord would cook the meat they had bought for themselves, and maybe sell them bread for the journey next day.

The whole town was a vibrant market place, so keen to do business with all who came that the bishops were regularly obliged to punish illegal Sunday trading. But despite the apparent prosperity, or perhaps because of the great increase in traffic that it brought, Gloucester's roads were notoriously bad. Not only the hapless 'Doctor Foster' had trouble with them: the men of the city remembered to their shame that Edward I's horse had floundered deep in their mud and the king had refused to visit the place again. The Bristol Road out to the south was in an appalling state when Sutton came, so bad that the previous year the bishop of Worcester, whose responsibilities extended as far as Bristol, had offered indulgences for its repair.[6] The streets of the town itself were little better. To the mud and filth of any medieval town with a large butchers' quarter and livestock fair, were added the mess that comes with a busy trading place and crossroads, the silt of the Severn and the unpleasant connotations of the 'Fullbrook Stream' that flowed, or overflowed, by the north gate as it drained the public latrines. By 1434, things had come to a head and a royal tollage grant was made for Gloucester to begin paving some of its streets, but that was of no benefit to Robert Sutton a decade before.

Leaving Gloucester and its sainted king behind, devout travellers paused to make an offering at the newly restored chapel of St Kyneburgh at the south gate. Since her translation to a new shrine in April 1390, a spate of miracles had been reported here, too, and her power to help suppliants was unquestioned. From the chapel, two roads led south past Llanthony Priory, to its east and west. The more westerly one, which led to the main gate, today heads out into a workaday industrial estate that hems in the old enclosure wall. But the juxtaposition is not so incongruous after all: how many heavy waggons of grain rumbled along this road to fill the monumental priory tithe barn in Sutton's day? And just beyond the surviving fragment of gateway, a wayside cross picked out in black bricks on the wall still blesses the traveller on his way, while the traffic crashes past.

From Llanthony, past Hempsted and Quedgeley St James, dodging the worst of the road's dereliction, Sutton went down onto what is the line of the old Roman road for a while. A brief diversion to cross the Frome by the ancient Fromebridge mill, another small river crossing at Cambridge, and then he headed more nearly south, up off the wet valley and entered the Cotswold edge at Cam.

Local names like 'Breakheart Hill' are hardly needed to highlight the change in landscape here, as he toiled up out of the Severn Vale. Dursley, however, was an important place and the main road came through the centre of the town. Time out of mind, its generous spring had been known for its healing properties, and by the fifteenth century it was also powering the fulling mills of a growing cloth industry. The Berkeley family had a small castle here, and the grand scale of the parish church of St James hints both at the significance of the cult of the spring and at the security and importance of the medieval town. Here there were several places where Sutton could spend the night. There was at least one religious house in Dursley: a small priory of nuns and perhaps also a friary of one of the less important Orders. But even failing these, a town with a healing spring, however local its fame, would have arrangements for welcoming pilgrims. If nothing else, Sutton could lodge with the parish priest, one of those innumerable candle-points of charity shining in his world.

From Dursley it was still a full day's walk to Bristol: six leagues of mixed countryside from steep wooded hills to the lowlands of the Severn and Avon. A full day's walk on legs that were beginning to be part of the penance. Bristol would represent the end of the first phase of the journey for Sutton: the end of the walk down the Severn beside which he had spent most of his life, the conduit of the materials of his livelihood. For one more day he was in broadly familiar territory, but after that he would be entering a world of new landscapes, new speech, new guardian saints.

Setting off early, with bread and hard cheese in his scrip for a meal on the way, and climbing over a stiff pair of hills, he came to North Nibley, where the church's newly carved nave corbels were demurely dressed in the fashions of the day. Then he plunged down the escarpment again, on 'a very irregular road through a large wood – Micklewood'.[7] The merest ghost of the wood survives today, although with some poetic justice a motorway service station has been named after it. One tree at least does survive, heroically so. The Tortworth Chestnut, just south of the parish church, is grown old beyond beauty and beyond reproach. For centuries it has been known as 'a remarkable Chestnut Tree . . . which by tradition is said to have been growing there in the Reign of King John; it is 19 Yards in compass [17 metres], and seems to be several Trees incorporated together'.[8] It was already a venerable specimen when Sutton came this way.

Down again onto the gentle undulating land closer to the rivers, through Cromhall and Tytherington St James, and suddenly every man Sutton spoke to knew that this was the Bristol Road. Just half a league more, and he was in sight of the gates, and confronted by a bewildering choice of places to stay. The best advice was probably the Benedictine St James's Priory, close by and especially sympathetic to Compostelan pilgrims, but there were plenty of other extramural houses: Greyfriars, Blackfriars, Whitefriars, the Whiteladies of the Magdalene nunnery and, down on the shoulder of land by the Avon, the Augustinian abbey.[9]

Of St James's, only the chapel remains today. But Sutton found a large and flourishing priory, in an extensive enclosure. Its chapel served the surrounding district as a parish church, and the monks were well used to accommodating travellers: their priory hosted three of Bristol's eight annual fairs on its land, and these combined happily with religious festivals that drew pilgrims to the city, especially for the priory's Feast of the Relics at Pentecost, and the big St James's fair on 25 July. For the latter, the prior was granted a levy of 3d. for every hogshead of wine unloaded in the port for the entire week. How kindly do the saints take care of their own!

Bristol was a robust and dynamic town with the legal status of a county, the first in England to achieve this level of independence. In terms of population and wealth, it was third in the land. To enhance their trade, the backbone of their prosperity, the citizens had diverted and altered the channels of the Rivers Avon and Frome, giving themselves safe deep-water quaysides. New areas had been taken in within the walls on both sides of the Avon, and the two parts of the town were linked by a spectacular stone bridge about sixty paces long. It was lined with merchants' houses three or four stories high, except in the middle where there was a gate with a chapel up above it, extending out well upstream and resting on a specially constructed extra pier. This Chapel of the Assumption was the wonder of all who saw it, and a potent symbol of Bristol's self assurance.[10]

Three times as populous as Worcester, and richer in proportion, Bristol was a bewildering experience even for the city-bred Sutton. Its chief source of income was the lucrative wine trade with Bordeaux. Wine was by far the biggest commodity in England's import trade, and Bordeaux still controlled most of the supply. Consequently, Bristol was booming, not least because the French wars made the voyage up the English Channel less safe, so that some of it was even transported overland to London.

The barrels of wine were hauled through the narrow cobbled streets on horse-drawn sledges, from quay to customs house to merchants' warehouses, and so on to wealthy private customers who bought by the barrel or by the waggon-load, and into the numerous taverns of a city as famous for its landladies and low-life as it was for its prosperous piety. Meanwhile, other cargoes were unloading: Icelandic cod, Basque iron, Castilian olive oil and dyestuffs, and barge-loads of surplus wheat coming down from the fertile Severn basin for redistribution or occasional export if a licence could be obtained. And ships were loading up too, from lighters full of the finished cloth that was the principal export through the city. This hive of activity went on all through the year, with hardly any lull for the poorer winter weather, although the new vintage each autumn brought an annual peak as the nobility competed for their supplies.

Bristol also benefited from another very particular trade, of a much more seasonal nature: the shipping of pilgrims to Compostela. As far back as the thirteenth century there are references to this lucrative business in the English state papers, and from 1361 onwards a more or less regular system was in place. Ship owners purchased a licence from the Royal Chancery, allowing them to carry a specified number of pilgrims on return tickets, under certain conditions. Thus on 27 April 1428, a licence was granted

> for William Coton, Jordan Sprynge and John Monke to take 100 pilgrims to St James in their ship the Mary of Bristol; provided they do not hinder the expedition of Thomas, earl of Salisbury, against the French, and that they do not take with them anything

harmful to the realm, any gold or silver in mass or money beyond
their reasonable expenses, nor reveal any secrets of the realm.[11]

The licence holders were thereby entitled to load up with some of
the many pilgrims who came to Bristol wanting to get to
Compostela without making the long journey overland. These
people were willing to pay for the privilege, at a time of year that
perfectly suited the shipmasters: the weather was less inclement and
the wine trade was relatively slack. They were shipped like so many
head of cattle down to the Spanish ports, given time to walk or ride
to Compostela and back, and then returned to Bristol.[12]

This pilgrim trade was, however, not without its risks. For all parties
there were the constant dangers of storm and wreck, as well as attack by
Breton, West Country and even Castilian pirates. For the shipmen, the
chief temptation was to pack in more pilgrims than the licence allowed,
and risk feeling the weight of the law; the sheriff and mayor of Bristol
were specially charged 'to enquire as to the owners and masters of ships
and vessels who are stated to have shipped at Bristol, and in the waters
of the Severne, a greater number of pilgrims for Santiago, and conveyed
them thither, than the king's licence allowed, to the king's prejudice,
and the deception of the court of his Chancery'.[13]

Sutton was also well aware that whatever perils he might be facing
on his long walk south, these pilgrims whom he met at Bristol, waiting
for a suitable boat, would have particular worries of their own:

Men may leve alle gamys,
That saylen to seynt Jamys!
Ffor many a man hit gramys [it tames]
When they begyn to sayl.
Ffor when they have take the see,
At Sandwyche, or at Wynchylsee,
At Brystow, or where that hit bee,
Theyr hertes begyn to fayl.

And some wold have a saltyd tost,
Ffor they myght ete neyther sode ne rost,
A man myght sone pay for theyr cost,

As for oo day or twayne.
Some layde theyr bookys on theyr kne,
And rad so long they myght nat se;
'Allas! myne hede wolle cleve on three!'
Thus seyth another certayne.

A sak of strawe were there ryght good,
Ffor som must lyg theym in theyr hood;
I had as lefe be in the wood,
Without mete or drynk;
Ffor when that we shall go to bedde,
The pumpe was nygh oure beddes hede,
A man were as good to be dede
As smell thereof the stynk.[14]

5

Salisbury's Patient Saint

From Salisbury to St Thomas Becket's Bridge, which has two
stone arches, is a mile wholly across open country. A pleasant
brook flows under this bridge, ... and enters the Avon about a
mile below Harnham Bridge ... From Salisbury to Romsey is
fourteen miles, and from there the road goes to Southampton.[1]

Sutton had never intended making the long sea voyage to Spain. But
any idea he may have had of finding a ship at Bristol that would take
him across the English Channel was quickly dashed. For the
Normandy ports he was recommended to try Southampton, while the
Breton captains of St Malo, though happy to trade, were no longer
prepared to take English passengers. Despite being allies, Englishmen

were at present most decidedly not welcome in St Malo. He could take a chance on a berth to a more westerly Breton harbour and make his way back east across Brittany overland, or he could go on to Southampton and wait there for a boat to Normandy. Brittany was a hesitant ally with an unfamiliar language; Normandy was ruled jointly with England and they were at peace. To Southampton he would go.

So now his road turned east, up the Avon valley towards the city of Bath. Not the main London Road that kept north of the Avon and soon entered the forest of Kingswood, but the road that crossed onto its southern bank, over the great Bristol Bridge. Through the inner gate guarded by the church tower shared by St John's and St Lawrence's, a two-minute walk through the early-morning city led to the High Cross,[2] where four more churches kept the pulse of old Bristol's heart: St Ewen's, St Werburgh's, Christ Church and All Hallows. Then down the High Street to St Nicholas's and the gate out beneath it, onto the magnificent bridge over the Avon that led to the newer district of Redcliffe. As big again as the old city, prosperous and much less densely populated, its southern boundary was marked in a great curve by high walls and a deep canal that the ingenious burgesses had made to carry the diverted river while their new bridge was built.

Beyond the Temple Gate, the Bath Road ran clear and clean before him. A good road, admittedly rather muddy in winter and dusty when dry, but a well-used link between the cities of Bristol, Salisbury and Southampton. Every month of the year, carts creaked along it, laden with luxury goods for the wealthy merchants of Bristol. Since the 1421 peace with Genoa, some of the best guarded loads came from their Southampton colleagues who had cautiously re-opened trade with the Italians in their huge carracks and galleys. Lying in the sheltered waters until late March, their cargoes were gradually dispersed, by specialist carriers and occasional packhorse trains: woad, madder and alum for dyeing; wax, blacksoap, silk and spices; almonds, oil, wine and the best Corinth raisins.[3] And in the other direction, accompanying Sutton on his way, went the Gascon wines from Bristol, to its thirsty hinterland.

It was a good road, wide enough for two carts to pass in comfort, and by and large a safe one. Henry V had brought a brief but most welcome respite from domestic lawlessness, and his contemporaries knew it: 'the pese at home and law so wele conserved, Wer rote and hede of all his grete conqueste'.[4] A good road it was, but not necessarily an easy one to take. There comes a point, perhaps, in every pilgrimage, once the novelty has worn off, when motivation falters. It is the first of many unexpected temptations along the way. Leaving the company of other pilgrims at Bristol, men and women who might be to Compostela and back again before he had even reached France, was desperately hard. Why do it this way, the slow, hard way, with the incessant moving on each day, with petty goals, small ambitions that seemed too insignificant to add up to anything worthwhile? Why go on alone from day to day, on an uncertain quest? Could he be sure that his penance would be enough? This low point of physical resilience fed the spiritual malaise. Why set his sights on far-distant Compostela? The Holy Blood of Hailes had already been left many leagues behind, unvisited. Kingswood Abbey too had been passed by, with its shrine of the Virgin that drew people from as far away as Scotland. All this day could offer was the drudgery of four leagues closer to the coast, a halt with the Austin and Victorine Canons at Keynsham, and a night at Bath.

Bath at least had a long tradition of caring for the footsore, aching and dispirited: '... the water ... springeth up in dyvers places of the citee. And so there beeth hoote bathes, that wascheth of teteres, other sores and scabbes.'[5] The cathedral priory had two dependent hospitals, one an extramural lazar house that had become a shelter for the destitute, the other, St John the Baptist by the public baths, founded particularly for the succour of poor travellers of both sexes who wished to use the healing waters. In the matter of relics and shrines, however, the city was remarkably barren. The priory had made an attempt to interest people in its new image of the Trinity, but with little success. The outspoken Agnes, wife of Thomas Cold the baker of Norton St Philip, was even heard to declare it was 'a waste of time to offer to the Trinity of Bath', and though she was hauled up before the bishop's court and made to recant, no doubt others shared her views.

The two small public baths stood either side of the hospital, the water 'the colour of deep blue sea water, and it churns continually like a boiling pot, giving off a somewhat unpleasant and sulphurous odour'. The Cross Bath particularly 'has alleviated many skin conditions and pains' and a wallow in its warm waters was a strange but soothing sensation.[6] Around the baths, meanwhile, the city also bubbled and churned. A long-festering litigation between priory and corporation had only just been settled in the royal courts, and one of the late King's last acts had been to demand that the bailiffs move decisively to arrest those gathering in the city taverns to make 'rancour dissension and discord.'[7] A city that for centuries had attracted the disabled and distressed was bound to encourage the discontented as well.

Sutton left Bath the same way as he had come in: out through the south gate and over the meadows to the bridge 'of five fine stone arches'. Then the suburb of Mary Magdalene and up 'a craggy hill full of fine springs of water'.[8] A fine hill, with fine springs no doubt, but a grim hill to climb on a damp April morning, with protesting hips and shins demanding a day's respite. Up to the top and then down again even more steeply, on a knee-jarring descent to the Midford Bridge, on the main road again.

That same main road ran close to the Carthusian Charterhouse of Locus Dei at Hinton: a deeply tempting proposition to call a halt there and seek refuge with the lay brothers and find some temporary stability and tranquillity. But with the day barely half over, it was too soon to stop. Or was it? Bodies have their own ways of imposing their agenda, of making their needs known. Just at the bottom of the next little valley, the sturdy market town of Norton came into view, the church of St Philip and St James nestling down by the brook, and there at the roadside was the George Inn. Newly built by the Hinton Charterhouse, it functioned both as a wayside inn and as a staple or clearing house for their surplus produce. To turn aside from the road for refreshment was the work of a moment; to take a bed for the night was a delight.[9] Town and inn between them provided restoratives of every kind: ale and bread, and Mass in the morning. On May Day the town would be buzzing for the patronal fair, but for now it went about its business with sober deliberation, as if mindful of the quiet piety of its Carthusian neighbours on the hill.

Another half-day's journey took Sutton to Warminster. A short Sunday pilgrimage with a late start after Mass and an arrival at midday, seeking the balance between sloth and pride. Both of them sins, both pitfalls on a pilgrimage, but hard to steer a course in between. The pains in his legs kept the beat of his thoughts, until the road curved in past St Denys and he was there.

Warminster presented its older face to the west, its new houses extending eastwards along the High Street and Market Place. Despite the best efforts of bird and beast, traces still lingered on a Sunday from the big weekly Saturday corn market, a 'pitched' market where the sellers tipped a sample of their grain out for inspection onto the wide street. With twelve-score carts lumbering in on a good week, and buyers converging from all over the region, the town's prosperity was solidly based. The Bell and the Red Lion, and three dozen other inns, fed and quenched the thirst of hundreds of customers, creating their own demand for grain in the process. By Sunday afternoon, the rush was over, sellers and purchasers departed, and the town dozed snug beneath its thatch, waiting for the weekly cycle to begin anew.

Accommodation was not hard to find for a Sunday night, and refreshment too at a price. A good rest would at least make the next stage of the journey tolerable: seven leagues to Salisbury, the next city on the high road, and gentle going by all accounts. For once there was no doubt of the way: the River Wylye joined the road soon after Warminster, and stayed with it to the end. In fact, there were two roads, one each side of the broad, flat-bottomed valley; the old one to Wilton on the south, the more frequented one to the north. Numerous summer fords linked the villages strung out along them, and even in winter the dilettante river could be crossed with care. Past the Langfords, the southern slopes of the valley were clothed in the trees of Groveley Forest, which extended right to the walls of Wilton. Within the Forest lay Wishford Magna, recently inherited by young Thomas Bonham. Despite living a quiet life, more withdrawn from public affairs than his late father, he was destined to create an enduring legend. Delaying his marriage until 1440, his wife then remained barren for nine years, before producing nine children so swiftly that she was soon believed to have given birth to twins and septuplets, with 'a confident tradition that these seven children were all baptised at the font in this church, and that they were brought thither in a kind of chardger [a large dish].'[10] Within the church, two effigies show Thomas's grandparents, dressed in the sober styles of late-fourteenth-century minor gentry.

Sutton, meanwhile, trudged on down the valley. One league remained to Wilton, then another to Salisbury. And after a long day, the leagues were very long. Suddenly the prospect of gentle St Edith at Wilton seemed irresistible. There were bridges over the river, hospitals and an abbey in the town, and the hovering vision of prayers and professional care for a battered body.

The twin bridges over the Wylye led to Burdens Ball suburb. But what a contrast with Warminster. Wilton was a town dying on its feet. Several plots were newly vacant, their stones carted away and the rest returning to the dust; the Market Place was fallen into decay. No new tenants could be found for the row of eight purpose-built shops beneath the Guildhall, despite repeated rent reductions. There should have been a market on a Monday, but so few stall-holders could be persuaded to pay even a modest fee that it was no longer viable. Only West Street, leading back up the valley towards Wishford, was still recognizable as part of a once-flourishing ancient borough.

The reason for Wilton's decline was simple: New Sarum, just an hour away, was competing vigorously and successfully with its cloth trade, its markets, and above all its bridge. Ever since Old Sarum was relocated to Salisbury, it had pressed for more than the Tuesday market it had been granted, and soon Wilton's ancient rights to three markets a week gave way in the face of strenuous poaching by its assertive new neighbour. The *coup de grâce* was struck when the bishop built Harnham Bridge, effectively diverting traffic and trade coming up from the south into his new city, and leaving Wilton high and dry. 'Before this was done, Wilton had twelve or more parish churches and was the principal town in Wiltshire.'[11]

Wilton had only one remaining string to its bow and by Sutton's time it was being used with determination. Wilton had St Edith. Her story had just been published in rough local verse, the author begging for divine aid

> ... *to brenge to godde heyndynge,*
> *Jhesu, for seint Edus sake,*
> *Thys werke that y, so unconnynge,*
> *Presumpswyslyche have undere-take.*

A daughter of the Saxon King Edgar and a Wilton girl, Edith spent most of her short life at the abbey there, where her mother had become abbess. As was the way with pious Saxon royalty, she was acknowledged as a saint in her lifetime, and a cult grew up:

> *So falle hit by this mayden, seynt Ede,*
> *That mekeness and lowenes dud hurre so encresse*
> *That in hurre lyffe, as we done rede,*
> *Gret miracles he dud thoro goddys grace*
>
> *... So mony myraclus for hurre god wrought*
> *To every mon that ony nede hadde,*
> *Of ony bone that hurre ryghtwyslyche bysought:*
> *He had anone what ever he badde.*[12]

With such a powerful patroness, it was not unreasonable to hope that the fortunes of the abbey, and with it the whole town, might yet be saved. Many of the town churches, and several of the bridges, were in a parlous state, but the abbey at least was showing some signs of returning prosperity. Although down to 40 nuns, a pale shadow of its former royal glory, it was still a relatively wealthy place. The archbishop's inspection of 1423 found everything restored to good order under the indomitable Abbess Christine, who also ruled over a college of 16 clergy who served the numerous altars in the abbey church.

Out in the town, the decline in trade had affected the hospitals as well. The old lazar house of St Giles now catered for the occasional destitute traveller as well as any remaining lepers who might need help, and St John's had become a hospital for poor men. At the abbey gates,[13] the Magdalene was an almshouse for 12 old men, in return for their prayers for the soul of St Edith. In the abbey guesthouse, however, Sutton still found a warm welcome. A clean bed, perhaps even one to himself, and an ample meal. A footbath to soothe his aching and blistered feet, and angelica to ease his rebellious legs, these were the ministrations of angels.

Morning brought early Mass at St Edith's tomb, an offering worthy of the comfort she brought, and the short road to Salisbury.

Pilgrim tokens were also for sale: pewter and lead badges of a Saxon princess in a wimple, holding her holy book. For her, the road to sainthood had been short and long ago, but her work of encouragement on earth continued. Popular acclaim had assured her a place among the elect, and her God had shown his approval.

How different from Wilton was Salisbury. A new cathedral city, just 200 years old, the tombs from Old Sarum on the hill reverently repositioned in its precincts. The new city hummed with life, its streets drained and clean, its Tuesday market doing a roaring trade, its cloth business supreme. But its holy man, Osmund the founder-bishop of Old Sarum, friend of the Conqueror, careful administrator and gentle calligrapher, was still not officially a saint. The hurt to civic pride was intense. Despite numerous miracles over many years, the popes continued to resist Salisbury's pleas to have Osmund canonized. Robert Levyng of Salisbury testified that in 1419 the young son of Robert Bulke the tailor had drowned in the river, and had revived after invocations to Osmund. And Sir Walter Rouse had been thrown by his horse and dragged helplessly caught in his stirrups until freed by the intervention of the holy bishop.[14] Osmund revived dead children, cured toothache, paralysis and insanity, and still his canonization was delayed. Local people came to the green marble tomb topped with his noble effigy, and reached through its openings to be close to their saint, but without wider recognition their numbers were small and their offerings meagre. One day, justice would be done and Salisbury's patient saint would be acknowledged by all.[15] For now, an inscription extolling the glories of his episcopate was the best the city could give him.

Salisbury Cathedral had no associated monks, so lacked the full facilities of a priory. There were plenty of inns in the city, but pilgrims could also stay at St Nicholas's Hospital at Harnham Bridge. Despite the trend towards long-term almshouse accommodation, there were a few beds there for travellers, especially if they could make a donation towards the upkeep of the bridge. The hospital and associated inn and chapel on the bridge were run by a non-resident warden, one Master Richard Bucklehurst, and three chaplains who were to be seen about town in their distinctive uniform of russet cloaks. The permanent residents participated in the full round of daily worship in their own chapel, but passing pilgrims were free to come and go as they pleased.

St Nicholas was an opportune saint to shelter with at this stage of the journey. Protector of bridges and river crossings, he had a care for all travellers, and especially those at sea. As the English part of the pilgrimage drew to a close, and thoughts turned towards the Channel crossing, Nicholas was a good companion. And Osmund, on his long road to sainthood with no end yet in sight, was something of a comfort, too.

*

From Salisbury over Becket's Bridge, the high road passed through the remnants of Clarendon Forest, its trees barely yet bursting into leaf. Most of the Forest was enclosed, and managed by the struggling little Ivychurch Priory. Once clear of the Forest, the road began to rise steadily, until at the very crest of the hill Sutton found the smaller road he was looking for, branching off to the left along the escarpment edge, with sweeping views over the broad valley below. The chalky soil was sticky and slippery, but at least there were no floods up there, and progress was steady if difficult. After a couple of hours, the road dropped diagonally down the scarp, into Lockerley and so to the Austin Canons at Mottisfont, in their priory nestling down by the River Test.

Mottisfont had two quite different focuses for devotion. It had its own local saint, Peter de Rivallis, their founder's brother, who was known as 'the holy man in the wall' for the prayers that were answered at the site of his tomb. It also possessed a most sacred relic, venerated as the actual finger of John the Baptist, with which he had first pointed to Christ.[16] What more precious talisman could there be, than to go abroad strengthened by the sight of the finger that showed the way to God?

6

By Sea from Southampton

Kepte than the see about in specialle,
Whiche of England is the rounde walle;
As thoughe England were lykened to a cite,
And the walle enviroun were the see.
Kepe than the see that is the walle of Englond,
And than is Englonde kepte by Goddes sonde [grace].[1]

A maritime nation, England was enriched and guarded by the sea. But by the same token, she could be vulnerable to seaborne attack. To flourish, she needed a vigorous foreign policy and confident seamen, as surely as a healthy soul depended on proper living. Crossing Hampshire to Southampton, Sutton saw at first hand the effects of the French wars on life in coastal areas. Many of the Mottisfont priory lands were close to the sea, and had been 'frequently invaded by Flemings, French and Normans and other enemies of the realm, for the defence of which men-at-arms from time to time lodged at the priory, consumed its animals and grain and carried away as booty other of its movable goods, wherefore the cultivators of the said fields had left them for the most part uncultivated.'[2]

The same ambiguity typified Southampton itself. Its virile trade demanded open access to the sea, but it was thereby laid open to all manner of piratical attacks. In 1338, right at the start of the wars, the town had been surprised by a French raid while the populace were at Mass, and many houses were burnt to the ground. The French returned in 1377, and after this a more determined effort at fortification got underway. A town ditch was dug, the ruined castle partly rebuilt, and haphazard attempts were made to build walls. The appearance of a hostile Genoese fleet off the Isle of Wight in

June 1416 concentrated local minds, but the work was only completed in 1418–19, with repairs and alterations to the King's New Tower and God's House Gate. Every improvement to the seaward defences met with dogged opposition from the merchants, who foresaw loss of income if their customary private access points to the quays were stopped up.

Southampton had a long history of resolute wealthy merchants. One such was Gervase Le Riche de Hampton, who long ago had founded 'God's House' to accommodate the travellers he had been in the habit of lodging in his own house. Under the aegis of St Julian, patron saint of poor travellers and good innkeepers, it stood in the south-east corner of the town, and its staff of priests and laypeople cared for needy seafarers, travellers and pilgrims. Here, those arriving by sea and those hoping to find a berth could spend a night and get their bearings. Damaged in the French raids, God's House had finally been rebuilt and refurbished in 1417 and was now fully open for business again, drawing rent income from its many properties in the town. It had a hall each for its male and female inmates, and a single large chapel,[3] and as well as sheltering travellers overnight, it regularly dispensed alms to paupers at the gates.

In mid-April, there was plenty of shipping activity, and plenty of business on the quays. It was only a matter of time before a suitable vessel could be found, making a passage to one of the Norman ports from which the roads ran south. Meanwhile, there was a space for Sutton to regroup, restore body and soul, and attend to some legal matters. His documents checked and declared in order, a permit was made out by the Southampton authorities as one of the ports entitled to deal with pilgrim licences, and the statutory fee of 6d. paid. With these conditions fulfilled, 'all manner of people, as well clerks as others' might cross the seas as pilgrims with the goodwill of the King. Without them, confiscation of all his goods would surely follow detection. Once a ship was found, a price could be negotiated with the master, if he did not find one eager to help a pilgrim for the benefit of his own soul.

The last of the vessels that had lain off Southampton through the stormy season were preparing to depart, laden with Wiltshire cloth, blankets, bales of raw wool, pewter and fine Nottingham alabaster carvings. In their place, the smaller coastal vessels of the home merchants were busy, some loading goods to distribute to the smaller Channel harbours, while others brought in the West Country tin and lead that the Italians were so eager to buy. Since 1410, Thomas Middleton's new Town Quay at the Watergate had operated a commercial crane, at a charge of 5d. a tun for wharfage, cranage and lighterage combined. Whether the merchants of Salisbury liked it or not, the charges were passed on to them, and Southampton, keeping its new crane and wharf in prime working order, benefited from a swifter throughput of goods.

Even with efficient new methods like these, it could still take many weeks to turn around a vessel. Unloading, assessing for Customs, selling, making new deals, honouring old ones, transferring goods from warehouse to hold, refitting and revictualling, all this took time. A swifter passage might be made on one of the many little balingers servicing the army in France, *The Gabrielle, La Faucoun, Le Swan,* that seemed to fly back and forth across the sea. Some as small as 20 tuns made regular crossings, dwarfed by the royal 'great ships' like the 500-tun *Trinity Royal* with her crew of 300, and the newly built giant *Gracedieu,* a massive 1,400 tuns, 70 paces stem to stern. What the balingers lacked in size, they made up for in number and speed. Granted, they were unable to do much against an unfavourable wind, but downwind they were hard to beat, carrying charter passengers, reinforcements, dispatches and all manner of supplies from goose quills for the fletchers to corn and herrings under licence to supplement army stores.

Riding at anchor in Southampton Water was a fleet of royal ships, waiting to be sold off into private hands as the navy was wound up to pay off the late King's debts. Among them was the *Holyghost of Spain,* a Castilian prize previously called the *Santa Clara of Spain.* The crew, armaments and the ship's dog had been returned to Spain, but the *Santa Clara* herself was retained, and rebuilt at Southampton. She had emerged as a two-masted vessel of 290 tuns and served with Henry V's navy for his Normandy campaign, taking part in the engagement off Harfleur in 1416, when the combined Franco-Genoese fleet was scattered and three of their huge carracks were brought back in triumph to Southampton. Now the *Holyghost* was to be bought by her master Ralph Huskard and three other Southampton men, for £200, and

Huskard intended using her on a pilgrim trip to Compostela. Among the smaller royal ships were two that were ready to sail at short notice: the *Katherine Breton*, a balinger prize captured in 1417, which had been snapped up for £20 by John Starling of Grenwich on 5 March, just two days after the sale was ordered; and the *Craccher* of 56 tuns, built in 1417 and known to be in good condition, whose sale for £26. 13s. 4d. to three Devon mariners was confirmed on 30 April.[4] Somewhere among all these vessels a passage to Normandy would be found.

Once a berth was secured, all that could be done was to find lodgings in the town, and wait for cargo, wind and tide. Finding suitable accommodation in a busy port was not so easy, but St Julian's had limited space, and a constant stream of poorer pilgrims than Sutton came into Southampton on their way to the shrines of England. Legislation to control the worst excesses of the innkeepers had limited effect, and pilgrims were still liable to be caught 'spending their goods upon vicious hostelars, which are oft unclean women of their bodies.'[5] With good fortune, a comfortable bed could be found for a penny a night, and food for a further 2d. But what with the armies of fleas, and other bedfellows who might wish to talk far into the night, or who snored, or prematurely extinguished the candle (*in extremis* by throwing the chamber pot over it), and who might in any case rob you once you were asleep, a peaceful night was far from guaranteed.

At least there was plenty to see to while away the long days of waiting. To all the trades of any borough were added the novelties of a thriving coastal port, the cloth carts coming in and the exotic items in the grocers, spicers and chandlers: luxurious cloth of gold, silks, oriental gold work and jewelry cheek by jowl with more workaday goods. St Mark fell on a Sunday in 1423, so there was no extra holiday, but there was the new Great Festival of St George, instituted after the victory at Agincourt. On its eve the populace came out onto the streets for the afternoon, and the young men shot at the butts outside the northern walls, while the taverns did brisk business. On Sundays and on the festivals, it was the women's turn, parading their latest fashions for their neighbours to envy. Southampton tailors were prosperous and well organized, with their own guild since 1406, and their trade increased 'from the alien folk coming into the port of the said town in carracks, galleys, ships of Spain, Portugal, Germany, Flanders, Zealand, Prussia, and others, who at their arrival there were wont for their use to have their cloths cut out by the tailors of the said town.'[6] All those foreigners added to the Babel of strange tongues in the bustling streets, the merchants of London and Wiltshire contrasting with the dominant Hampshire dialect, and all equally unintelligible to unattuned Worcestershire ears.

The crossing might be over in two days, or it might take a week or more if the weather turned foul. So it was hard to know how much food to buy before leaving, although most first-time sailors found they didn't want to eat at all until they were on dry land again. The combination of shallow draught and broad beam produced a peculiarly uncomfortable motion, the horror of all landsmen. Offering for a calm crossing was probably the best preparation. A passenger on a merchant ship had a space allocated on deck, with temporary canvas walls erected to keep off the worst of the spray, and a view of the rearing sail and the tossing sea. And there he would remain, the butt of seamen's jokes whether he visited the side or not, until land was reached.

> *Anon the mastyr commaundeth fast*
> *To hys shyp-men in alle the hast*
> *To dresse hem sone about the maste,*
> *Theyr takelyng to make.*
> *With howe! hissa! then they cry,*
> *'What, howe, mate! thow stondyst to ny,*
> *Thy felow may nat hale the by'*
> *Thus they begyn to crake [hector].*

> *A boy or tweyn anone up styen,*
> *And overthwart the sayle-yerde lyen; –*
> *'Y how! taylia!' the remenaunt cryen,*
> *And pulle with alle theyr myght.*
> *Bestowe the boote, Boteswayne, anon,*
> *That our pylgrymes may pley theron;*
> *For som ar lyke to cough and grone*
> *Or hit be full mydnyght.*[7]

In ideal conditions, the voyage from Southampton to Normandy might indeed be accomplished in little more than a day, and of this time only a few hours might be out of sight of all land. But many things could happen to prolong the voyage, and many dangers might be encountered on the way. The wind was unreliable, and might fade away or change, so a straightforward passage could suddenly become a desperate battle to return to port, or to find another safe haven before being swept far off course with no chance of beating back into the teeth of the wind. It was not uncommon for ships to venture out and then spend days offshore, unable to go either on or back, while supplies ran low and rigging frayed:

> *At first, when we left England, we had only food and drink and fodder for four days, for if we had had a good wind we should have sailed from England to Brittany in four days, but we were seventeen days on our way . . . There we lifted our horses out of the ship, but they could neither stand nor go.*[8]

Even if the Channel crossing was good, the final approaches to harbour were not guaranteed. Cherbourg, the port nearest to Southampton, offered a relatively easy approach with few reefs to avoid, but with wind against tide it produced infamous choppy seas and, should the wind fail, there were horrors to either side. Eastward, the coast curved round to the old rock-bound harbour of Barfleur, where the *White Ship* had foundered long years ago, taking with her the pride of England.[9] To the west, past cliffs and coves, it suddenly turned at a high cape and the sea boiled into the Alderney Race, where no small vessel was safe. The best hope then would be to creep on down the coast and hope to make landfall at some little harbour farther south.

These natural perils apart, there was the ever-present risk of hostile shipping. West Country pirates might be busy elsewhere, but their Breton cousins were a constant nagging fear. Above all, the Castilians were now active in northern waters, and in league with England's enemies: in March 1421 a detachment had appeared in mid-Channel, and had only been chased away when a hastily assembled squadron of 13 Southampton ships sailed out to challenge them. And on 29 January 1423, a balinger commanded by one Christopher Huet had to put out from Cherbourg, manned by members of the royal garrison, to aid a little Poole-based scaffa that was sighted coming under attack from a pirate balinger from St Malo.[10] The safe keeping of the seas never seems a wiser policy than when you are helpless upon the ocean.

The best outcome by far for Sutton would be to wake in the morning after one night at sea, and see the high hills behind Cherbourg, and the gap where the river came down to the harbour, beside the strong castle and town walls. Then it would not be long before he was standing unsteadily on the quay, asking directions to the Maison-Dieu in the suburbs. Cherbourg had become the main port and garrison for western Normandy, and was a safe place to be. Held briefly by the French until recaptured after a protracted siege in 1418, the castle and walls were rebuilt, a main street renamed after the victorious Duke Humfrey of Gloucester, and even the suburbs on the sandy flats to the south were rising from the ashes. Everywhere, English voices were heard. As well as the 160-man garrison, merchants and craftsmen were taking up the generous offers of tenements and workshops in the town, replacing those Normans killed or scattered by the siege. Mixed in with them, there were plenty of Normans too; people who had held to their English allegiance through the two decades of French rule, or who had wearied of the bloodshed and were willing to take the oath to King Henry, or women who had married English soldiers and were already beginning a new race of Anglo-Normans.

Out on the promontory, hard up by the stout seaward walls that had proved so difficult to breach in the siege, the Church of the Holy Trinity was being rebuilt. Work had begun ten years previously, and now was continuing in earnest, using fine Caen stone brought round by sea to the basin nearby. Within the nave, a series of 17 bas-reliefs originating in Sutton's lifetime epitomize his world: the insecurity of the times and the deeper certainty that underpinned it. In a poignant *Danse Macabre*, Death skips around a church as lovingly built as Holy Trinity would one day be. Death the ultimate leveller smiles into the face of bishop and burgess, and walks with beggar and king. With pirates and storms at sea, wars and disease on land, Sutton's generation was as profoundly aware as any other before or since that life and prosperity are temporary phases in the greater scheme of things.

> *What helpith now the stat in which I stood*
> *To rewle cites or Comouns to governe.*
> *Plente of richesse or increce of good*
> *Or old wynnyng that cometh to me so yerne.*
> *Deth al defaceth so who list to lerne*
> *Me for tareste he comyth on so faste*
> *Eche man ther-fore shold a-fore discerne*
> *Prudently to thynk upon his laste.*[11]

PART III

Normandy

7

South from Cherbourg

Where formerly there were a hundred and eighty domestic hearths, now there are only sixteen.[1]

The old road from Cherbourg climbed steeply from the narrow coastal plain, between lowering crags. A short stiff climb, twisting up until the city was laid out far below: the river, the sheltered harbour, the newly repaired castle and walls, and beyond them the shifting sand-dunes and the sea that was the way home to England.

Turning his back resolutely, Sutton took his first clear look at the way south, which ran through the intimidating Forest of Brix, spread out in waves before him, and then, somewhere on its far side, through the marshes of the Marais. Together, these twin barriers all but cut off Cherbourg from the rest of Normandy beyond. There were few roads to choose from and none of them was safe, in a peninsula ravaged by three generations of grief.

Seventy-five years earlier, the Great Pestilence had come, after two years of foul weather and a murrain that laid low crops and cattle. Afflicted villages wore a black flag on their church towers, and the dead buried the dead. Some communities had died completely; most lived on, much reduced, to recount the horror. In 14 years the plague had returned, striking in recurrent waves: now at the heads of households, leaving orphans and widows, now at babes in arms. But this much was the common experience of Worcestershire as well. Normandy had suffered worse, with invasions and civil war. With Cherbourg in English hands, supported by the Navarrese King

Charles II ('The Bad' to the French), the frustrated French had adopted a scorched-earth policy and razed the crops of the peninsula. For 'Fire gilds War as the Magnificat adorns Mattins', as one warlord proudly declared.[2] Or, as we might more cynically say, 'Arson is the icing on the cake of war.'

Lessay Abbey is a reminder of how little we change. Pillaged and burnt out by the Navarrese in 1356, it stood in ruins for 30 years before the money was found to rebuild it. Just finished in time for the traumas of the Lancastrian invasions, it survived successive wars thereafter, only to be mined and blown apart by the retreating Germans in 1944. Rebuilt again, its honey-warm walls breathe forgiveness for the stupidity of men.

Back in the Middle Ages, the armies plundered and pillaged, and the peasants starved. Drought followed flood, pestilence returned. The King of France lapsed into insanity, and civil war brewed, with Armagnac and Burgundian factions alike appealing to England for aid that never came. The nobility of Normandy hedged their bets, and sent one son into each camp, while the others took to the forests and did best of all, as brigand chiefs. The roads, unmaintained and unsafe, led between terrified towns. Even the best-fortified cities abandoned their hinterlands: 'there are many notable and ancient highways, bridges, lanes and roads, which are much injured, damaged or decayed and otherwise hindered, by ravines of water and great stones, by hedges, brambles and many other trees which have grown there, and by many other supervening hindrances, because they have not been maintained and provided for in time past; and they are in such a bad state that they cannot be securely used on foot or horseback, nor by vehicles, without great perils and inconveniences; and some of them are entirely abandoned because men cannot resort there.'[3] No wonder, then, that when Henry V of England came, offering peace to 'His Duchy', many welcomed him. Their numbers reduced to a third in three generations, the survivors of the holocaust of Normandy began to live again.

The Forest of Brix reached from the east coast of the peninsula almost to the west, and from Cherbourg to Valognes. Bisected by the old Roman road, it had been surrounded by 50 prosperous villages, whose people used its timber for fuel and building, its acorns for their pigs. But most of the people were now gone, their farms nothing but brambles and thorns, their fields a wasted scrubland. Only the wolves did well. They flourished in the abandoned forests and ventured out into the farmland, picking off the sheep left shepherdless. Sutton had never seen a wolf in his life. It was England's proud boast that she had 'schepe that bereth good wolle … and fewe wolves; perfore the schepe beeth the more sikerliche with out kepynge i-lefte in the folde'.[4] Wolves were an object of loathing, and rumours were rife. They took prey living or dead, they fed on the earth, they even lived on air. They took babies from the cradle, ripped still-warm felons from the gallows, dug bodies from the grave. They 'were so hungry at this time that they came into the good towns at night and did a very great deal of damage, often swimming across the Seine and several other rivers. They used to go at night to country graveyards and dig up and eat newly buried corpses.'[5] With such desecrations to their name, it was easy to credit tales that they were not necessarily wolves at all. The devil was about in the wilds, and ran in lupine form. Never look a wolf in the eye.

King Henry, practical and prudent, had realized the threat to morale and the economy, and had appointed wolf hunters by royal warrant, to seek out and destroy these terrors of the forest. Raoul Dargonges in Cherbourg Vicounty and Degory Gamel in Carentan were the current officers for the Cotentin, and a levy of 2d. for each dog wolf caught, 4d. for bitches, was to be raised from each household of the afflicted communities, to pay them. 'For it has come to our notice that, since our wars and as a consequence of them, many wolves and other predatory beasts have greatly increased in our said Duchy and especially in our Vicounty of Chierebourc, so that they are devouring numerous human beings, oxen, cows, sheep and other livestock, as we have heard …'[6] Instead of executed criminals left hanging by the wayside as a warning to the populace, the bodies of wolves were now displayed and carried in triumph through village streets.

After only five years of English rule, however firm, Brix was still a place of many fears. The main road down to Valognes was well used, with mounted messengers and waggon trains relieving the loneliness and unnatural quiet, but to stray off it was to become lost in a maze

of overgrown tracks. Somewhere in the heart of the Forest, built to
succour benighted travellers, was the Priory de l'If, whose evening
bell rang out through the trees to guide wayfarers. But with coppices
left to grow wild, and assarts abandoned, there was no one to point
the way and little hope of finding it unaided. Better to hurry on along
the high road and pray that nothing untoward befell.

Coming to the end of the Forest at last, the roofs of Valognes
came suddenly into sight. A massive medieval castle guarded the
Cherbourg road and dominated the town, but could not save it in
time of war. Changing hands repeatedly with the ebb and flow of
armies, the town was burnt and rebuilt many times. But in March
1417, the castle had capitulated to the English without a struggle,
and the relieved townspeople, thoroughly sick of war, hastened to
pay homage to King Henry. With a garrison of 36 in residence,
under tight discipline, the town was secure. Now that the Final
Peace of 1420 was ratified, the soldiers were there to protect the
population from outlaws, not to subdue it, and were expected to
behave accordingly. They were required to wear the red cross of St
George at all times, so their profession was clear. They mostly
lodged out in the town and, unlike the French troops, they were paid
and fed. Unregulated foraging was forbidden, and those who stole
or offered violence to clergy or women faced the death penalty. By
such extraordinarily rigorous legislation, backed up by active
military courts, the English found grudging respect in many
Norman hearts.

Valognes was only a short day's walk from Cherbourg, but after
braving a wolf-infested forest it was a good place to spend the night,
with the town *en fête* for May Day. Besides, after a fortnight's
inaction at Southampton, and then the voyage, it was quite far
enough. The inn of St Michael regularly housed pilgrims, as did the
Priory of Ham and the Franciscan convent, while just outside the
town to the south, at Lieusaint, the chronically sick were lodged at
the old leprosy hospital of La Madelaine. It was a pleasant surprise
to find that neither language nor nationality was a barrier here:
goodwill and large numbers of English travellers ensured that
Sutton got what he needed, and could ask advice for the road ahead.
His next goal was Our Lady of Coutances, but how best to reach her?

Beyond Valognes, there were three roads through the Marais, a huge area of marshland along the river systems that flooded to a lake in winter and now at the beginning of May was just becoming passable. One swung west via the garrison town of St Sauveur-le-Viconte and so avoided all but the upper Douve wetlands. Another, which led to the main road to Paris, kept well to the east and crossed a series of boggy valleys on narrow causeways,[7] before crossing the river mouths near Carentan, by bridge or ford. But right down the middle of the peninsula there was a third road, smaller, but avoiding the worst of the marshes on either side. The Romans had chosen this route, and so did many medieval travellers. It was shorter, and led due south, following a ridge of higher ground like a long island in an inland sea.

A long day's walk down this road was Périers, at the far side of the marshes. Its church housed a precious relic whose festival was kept the very next day, which confirmed Sutton's choice of route. To be sure of reaching the town by nightfall meant an early start and little respite during the day. But at Orglandes, two leagues into the journey, he paused briefly at the old Church of Our Lady. The lands around were held by a firmly pro-English family, and the church itself was right on the road, so there was little to fear. Inside, a newly dedicated statue of St James joined the Lady in welcoming him and blessing him on his way.

Not every village was so friendly, and the road was not always quite straight. By the church and castle of Etienville, it came to an unexpected and abrupt end, down on the edge of a boggy valley. Where in summer a causeway led to a passable ford, there was nothing to be seen but the slowly drying mud of the Douve valley. So Sutton had to backtrack and go downstream a little to Pont l'Abbé, a bastide town at a newer and highly strategic crossing point. An army could be held up for a whole day if this route were sabotaged. A causeway a bowshot long, uneven and slick with mud, ran out across the drying mire to the bridge. All around, in the bowl of the valley, the last patches of land were emerging from the water, the trees shaking off winter's slime. At the height of the winter floods, the crossing would be made by ferry, in a flat-bottomed punt-like 'gabare', steered and propelled by a huge pole.

Once over the Pont l'Abbé bridge, the ground rose steeply up the valley edge, and after a slippery ascent Sutton regained the line of the old road, near the once-prosperous little monastery that watched over the ancient ford. Thereafter, as afternoon wore into early evening, the road blundered on past a succession of abandoned farmsteads, and careworn little settlements being patchily rebuilt by their impoverished inhabitants. Most of the houses were built of mud, the vivid orange clay of their walls luminous in the fading light and contrasting starkly with the roofs and wooden lintels. The road seemed to last for ever; pot-holed and rutted, with scrubby trees too close for comfort, it was an unpleasant ending to a long journey. St Jores, and then the ruined castle of Plessis Lastelle with more marshes visible down to the left, and then on again until at last he came upon the Great Road, wide and clear and safe-looking. And there to the left in the last of the light was Périers, into which he stumbled not a moment too soon.

8

The Cross, and
Our Lady of Coutances

Vox ultima Crucis.
Tarye no lenger; toward thyn herytage
Hast on thy weye, and be of ryght good chere.
Go eche day onward on thy pylgrymage;
Thynke howe short tyme thou hast abyden here.
Thy place is bygged above the sterres clere,
Noon erthly palys wrought in so statly wyse.
Come on, my frend, my brother most entere!
For the I offered my blood in sacryfice.[1]

Périers was an important little place. Small, but nursing a great treasure at its heart, where four straight roads met like the arms of a giant cross. Once, long ago, a Crusader had come homeward up the road from the east, bringing with him a piece of wood splintered from the True Cross. When he reached Périers, his horse had suddenly reared up, and refused to go on until his master understood that his relic was to be given to the church in this place and not at his home. At this, the bells of Périers were said to have rung for joy of their own accord.[2]

Festivals of the Cross were very important for Sutton. It was, after all, the means of grace and his best channel of love. As well as the commemorations of Holy Week, there was Holy Cross Day in September, and the newer Feast of the Invention of the Cross in May, which celebrated the finding of the Cross in Jerusalem by St Helena. All churches celebrated them, but to be in the presence of a portion of the True Cross on such a day was an opportunity not to be missed. Arriving in Périers on the eve of the festival, Sutton went into the lofty, candle-shadowed church with its shrouded reliquary of the Cross, then knelt before the lovely new statue of the Virgin and Child. Next morning, the quiet was no more and the church was alive with light and worship as the unveiled Cross was processed around for all to see.[3] Then the whole town erupted into a joyous third feast day in succession: May Day, then Sunday, and now this Monday festival as well. By evening, there would be no shortage of excitement among the young and the less reputable. It was just as well that Sutton, who might be misunderstood more readily than other strangers, wanted to be on his way before the morning was out:

> *La ne convient il demander*
> *S'ilz entrebatent quand sont yvres;*
> *Le prévost en a plusieurs livres*
> *D'amande toute au long de l'an.*[4]

Coutances was barely four hours away, first visible from Monthuchon down in the valley below. But then gradually the perspective changed, and as the road descended so the city with its newly repaired walls seemed to rise up until it was towering high above the river, on its craggy hill.

The city seemed happy with its English rulers. The new bishop, Pandulph, had clearly demonstrated his support for them and had encouraged his clergy to follow his lead. Where the parish clergy led, most of their flock would follow. Simple arrangements for submission had been put in place as soon as Normandy was reunited to the English Crown. The richest had to make individual submissions in person, but those with incomes of less than £60 a year could obtain a general pardon in exchange for an oath of allegiance to King Henry, and for a modest enough fee of 10d. they were issued with a sealed proof of their compliance.[5]

The only church of note within the walls, apart from the cathedral itself, was St Nicholas, tucked down below the main street near the gate. Badly damaged in earlier bouts of fighting, it was being rebuilt by its energetic curé Thomas du Marest. He was finding enough citizens willing to support his labours, and gifts of timber, stone, lime and sand kept coming in. In 1417, despite the uncertain political climate, he had had the faith to order a new stone statue of St Nicholas from the celebrated school of sculpture at Caen, for the considerable sum of 14 gold pieces (each valued at 30s.), and he had been fortunate to receive a donation of £21 earmarked to help transport the statue to Coutances.[6] The only sour note was that in 1420 the English had requisitioned his presbytery, forcing him to live in a smaller and less convenient house.

The cathedral at once dwarfed and blessed its city. Inside, the glowing red and blue glass told the stories of St George, St Thomas of Canterbury and St Blaise, patron of wool-carders and curer of sore throats. Time out of mind, there had been a pilgrimage to Our Lady of Coutances, who had once sat serene and immutable with the Child enthroned on her lap. She had been revered on her altar and processed round the cathedral on her feast days, healing many and accepting vows.[7] Within the memory of the oldest inhabitants, however, a new statue had been placed in the lady chapel, Our Lady standing holding the Child on her hip, with a gentle smile of sympathy for her suppliants. Thus she was now approachable, in tune with the spirit of the age; thus Robert Sutton made his prayers to her, and carried away with him an image of her when he moved on.

Outside the walls of the cramped city, down past the war-damaged church of St Pierre that was barely safe to enter, there was a Maison-Dieu where Sutton could spend the night. Situated as it was in the valley bottom, far below the cathedral,[8] it lacked the protection of walls and ramparts and had suffered considerably in the years of turmoil and war. But the rapid submission of the city to the English on this latest occasion had spared it much additional damage. Besides, it had been founded with such advantageous terms, all donors being granted an automatic one-seventh remission of their penances, that gifts of land had flooded in from all over the diocese and it was well placed to make a swift recovery when needed. It was run under the combined patronage of the Holy Spirit, Our Lady, St James, St John and St Antony, such a raft of holy protectors that both the hospital and its lodgers seemed sure to thrive. There was, in fact, some dispute over whether it had been founded by the bishop or by the Augustinians, perhaps not surprising in view of the large income to be administered.[9]

The Confraternity of the Holy Spirit who ran the Maison-Dieu included many notable men of the city, who viewed it as sheltered housing for their old age as well as an aid into the world to come, but it continued to offer accommodation to itinerants and pilgrims as well. On a feast day as important as the Invention of the Cross, Sutton might have hoped for a meal of fresh meat, but he was doomed to disappointment. The Maison-Dieu staff were claiming that their budget was so restricted by 'the wars and other misfortunes which have for so long troubled those regions and still afflict them now, that the poor who gather there daily cannot be fed, given drink, or be sustained in their other necessities ...'[10] If they were lucky, pilgrims might be given the basic Monday meal of bread, beans and some bacon, with cider or rough Normandy wine,[11] but otherwise they would have to try to buy their own bread up in the city. But whatever the disappointments and privations, Sutton at least spent this night safe under the protecting shadow of Our Lady of Coutances, well cared for, well lodged and well on his way across Normandy.

9

No Way to Mont St Michel

'Bien aimé Seigneur saint Michel, quelle était donc ton idée, lorsque tu bâtis dans la mer sauvage, et sur le Mont dans la mer? Kyrie Eleison.'[1]

At some point on his journey down through the Cotentin, Sutton received some very unwelcome news. It confirmed the rumours he had picked up back in Bristol, about St Malo being hostile to the English, but came as an unpleasant surprise nevertheless. Perhaps the Cherbourg officials who checked his licence to enter Normandy mentioned it, or perhaps another traveller warned him. He may not have been sure yet what effect it would have on his plans, but it was certainly true that the previous October, without any warning, a proclamation had been issued in the name of Henry VI:

> ... *nuls, de quelque estat ou condicion qu'ilz soient, ne voisent en pelerinage au Mont Saint Michiel, sur paine de confiscacion de corps et de biens. Et se vous trouvés aucuns qui, depuis les diz criz et publicacions aient faire le contraire, mettez iceulz es prisons du roy nostre dit souverain seigneur ...*[2]

Strong measures, but it seemed that the situation at Mont St Michel had become serious, and drastic action was needed. Despite the submission of Abbot Robert Jolivet, the few monks remaining on the island had refused to follow his lead. Instead, they had armed themselves and entrusted their defence to a lay leader, leaving the town dogs unchained by night to give warning of any imminent attack.

The Mount was the focus of one of the earliest and greatest pilgrimages of Christendom. People had converged there for centuries to do penance or to worship at the place where the Archangel had sanctified the earth. It was high on Sutton's list of shrines to visit, since Michael not only had power to halt the spread of disease, but he was invested with authority to weigh the souls of the dead at their judgement. Pilgrims approached him, therefore, with a strange mix of dread and hope, their lives quite literally hanging in the balance. Unfortunately for Sutton, Mont St Michel was also the centre of the French royal cult of St Michael and, as the weeks went by, it was fast becoming a focus for undercurrents of French disaffection with English rule, and a dangerous rallying point for Breton dissidents too. Abbot Jolivet had been granted the revenues of the Mount's estates for life; if the considerable pilgrim revenues could also be cut off, and a blockade enforced, this thorn in the side of the Duchy could be speedily removed. Thus, religious needs must give way to political necessity.

South of Coutances, the people were less enamoured of their new Lancastrian rulers. Perhaps because they had suffered less in the civil wars between the Burgundians and Armagnacs that had shredded the soul of France until 'no one ... could tell what rank was best – the great all hated each other, the middle classes were burdened with taxation, the very poor could not earn a living',[3] or perhaps because they were closer to Brittany and to the regions of France that had no folk-memory of being ruled from across the seas; whatever the reason, here the English were not loved. Of course, for most of the people most of the time, it made no difference who ruled: life was toil and tavern, fast and feast. But Sutton, as he tramped along the road that ran now straight as a measuring rod up hills and over valley causeways, now winding between villages in the untamed woods, began to feel the fragility of the Peace. The wayside taverns murmured with discontent. Tale-bearing and gossip were the bane of medieval life, high on the list of sins; whispering and slander have always been the stuff of sedition.[4] Whatever the propaganda might say, whatever the folk in England believed, the English grip on Normandy was not quite firm, and somewhere along the road this day Sutton passed into the area where it was least secure of all.

Offsetting the rancour of the natives was the immeasurably long tradition of pilgrim traffic to Mont St Michel. So well-established a route could not be erased by a mere change of government, and it was possible that a royal edict might be overlooked. In any case, there was little option but to press on southwards, and see what transpired. With all his credentials in order, Sutton could feel reasonably confident of obtaining justice in the end. The worst that was likely to happen was that he would be turned back at the shore.

All the way down this last stage to Genêts, the port guarding the way out to the Mount, a plethora of places offered lodgings to the converging pilgrims. On his route alone, Sutton had a choice of five Hôtels-Dieu and hospitals, including those at the appropriately named Repas and Chambres. Or he could continue past the St Maur hospital at Hocquigny and cross the ancient bridge over the little river in La Haye Pesnel, to the small Premonstratensian priory of St Jacques, which catered especially for pilgrims. Here indeed he was part of the purpose of the roads, in a place where for generations the 'Miquelots' had ebbed and flowed like the surging tides of the Bay.

The hinterland of Mont St Michel was also dotted with lazar houses, which at the height of the epidemic had sheltered hundreds of poor lepers. Whether these unfortunate living dead were drawn to the Mount in the hope of a cure, or whether they merely washed up like so much human flotsam at any place where rootless and hopeless people were regularly given charity, they had come in such numbers that the abbey eventually needed to found lazars for its own monks who had contracted the disease while tending them. In the old days, leper colonies of a hundred or more were not uncommon, but by Sutton's time it was rare to find one with more than a dozen residents. Terror of the disease had largely been diluted by the far greater trauma of the Great Pestilence, and fear, although usually mixed with careful charity, had largely given way to compassion. In England, leprosy had all but disappeared, and the occasional lepers that were encountered could be identified by the hand-bell they were obliged to carry when outside their colonies. But in France they were still quite often seen, carrying two pieces of wood fastened together with thongs to make a clapper. Thus they alerted other travellers to their condition, and begged for alms while keeping safely downwind.

A short league beyond the priory at La Haye Pesnel was La Lucerne Abbey, where English pilgrims were made especially

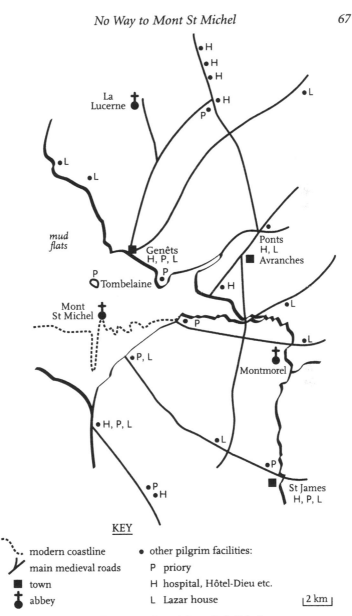

KEY

- • • • • modern coastline
- main medieval roads
- ■ town
- ✚ abbey
- • other pilgrim facilities:
- P priory
- H hospital, Hôtel-Dieu etc.
- L Lazar house

2 km

Pilgrim roads to Mont St Michel

welcome. Uniquely among the Norman abbeys, it had remained
stubbornly loyal to the English Crown from the far-off days when
the French king had driven King John out of his Duchy. Thus it had
acquired the sobriquet 'd'Outremer', signifying its allegiance to a
ruler across the sea. Now, with 'the whole duchie of Normandy
(Mont St Michel onlie excepted) reduced to the possession of the
right heire, which had been wrongfullie deteined from the Kings of
England ever since the daies of King John',[5] La Lucerne proudly
stuck to its nickname, proof of its faith in the ultimate triumph of
the English cause. It was well worth the extra hour's walk, worth
braving the stretch of desolate and derelict heathland to arrive at
this place for a night. Coming suddenly into view across its valley,
snug below its protecting hill, the grey-purple stones of the tower
seemed warm even on a chilly spring evening. Outside the
gatehouse was a covered porch where alms-bread was distributed
three times a week. But Sutton could pass within, to the guest house
and church beyond.

In fact, once inside, he found himself in a building site. La
Lucerne's staunch adherence to the English cause had made it a
frequent prey to French attacks and it had been badly mauled. Now
a restoration programme was well under way, and Sutton saw a
brand-new tower, a new nave from the windows up, and work in
progress on the gatehouse and many of the canons' private
buildings, with purple pudding stone and contrasting rich golden
granite brought from the abbey's own quarries nearby. In the
chapels, away from the workmen's noise, Sutton directed his prayers
especially to the Virgin, St Michael and the local saints Armel and
the blessed Achard.[6] Saint Armel in particular was noteworthy, with
a new statue recently put up in his honour. Born in South Wales, he
had settled in this area and not only saved men from shipwreck, but
he had once tamed a dragon and led it away with his stole around
its neck as a halter. As he was also known to be able to help sufferers
from headaches, fever and rheumatic pains of all kinds, he was an
invaluable ally for a pilgrim heading for lands where even dragons
might still exist.

In the next few days, however, the only dragons Sutton was likely
to encounter were the Welsh archers in the new garrisons around

Mont St Michel. The little coastal town of Genêts, from which the rocky island of Tombelaine and even the Mount itself seemed so tantalizingly close, was in a state of high alert. The River Couesnon, which normally flowed out to the west of Mont St Michel, had recently altered its course, so the rebels on the Mount were cut off by a deep channel carrying the combined waters of the three rivers of the bay.[7] Although this gave some additional protection to the garrison stationed out on Tombelaine, it made it much harder to know what was being planned. Ships from St Malo, in breach of the treaty between England and Brittany, were resupplying the besieged abbey, and at any moment an attack might be launched against the mainland.[8] Unlike the Mount, Tombelaine had been in English hands since 1418, and a force of mounted and foot lancers and over 50 archers under John Nessefeld were installed there, with the combined duties of watching the abbey defenders, keeping an eye on its dependent priory on Tombelaine and, now, also turning back any pilgrims attempting to cross the sands.

The priory and shrine of Our Lady of Tombelaine had an important tradition of its own. Many years ago, a woman heavy with child had been trapped by the rising tide on the sands near Tombelaine, and in her panic had gone into labour. Her prayers to St Michael, St John and, above all, to the Blessed Virgin were answered, the flood held back, and she and the newly born infant both escaped. A cross was erected on the sands between Tombelaine and the Mount to mark the spot where the miracle had occurred, and it had been maintained and restored ever since.[9] On the island, the small priory received a steady stream of pilgrims, who bought a badge of an enthroned Madonna of Tombelaine as proof of their visit. These pilgrims themselves might not have mattered greatly, but it was becoming clear to the English authorities that the Tombelaine outpost was giving very material aid to the mother-house. In July 1422 it had been discovered that 3,000 pounds of lead (over a metric tonne) had been removed from Tombelaine priory and spirited over to the Mount, almost certainly to be used to line a large new water cistern and help prepare the abbey for a protracted siege.

In the present situation, there was no possibility of Sutton being given permission to go to Tombelaine, let alone all the way to Mont

St Michel. All his carefully nurtured hopes of praying here to the Virgin and St Michael, which he had carried secretly with him for days, withered away. And with them went the stories he had heard of the treasures on the Mount, and the astonishing power that enabled such an abbey to cling to the face of such a rock. All this would have to remain in his mind's eye, supplemented only by descriptions from the inhabitants of Genêts. Deprived of their usual busy trade with the Mount, in food and cider and pilgrims, there were plenty of men idling about to tell him what he had missed.

Of course to get there you first had to brave the sands. Not for nothing was the abbey called 'St Michel In Periculo Maris'.[10] Many foolish pilgrims who knew nothing of the sea set off towards it unguided, not realizing that in a few hours the waters would cover this great muddy expanse. And as the tide came in, channels appeared, suddenly too deep to ford, cutting them off on ever-shrinking islands of despair. Or sometimes the sea mist rolled in, so they lost their way and wandered far out over the Bay, and were not heard of again unless the sea brought them in for burial many tides later.

But for those who made offerings at the Genêts priory, or at the Hôtel-Dieu chapel of St Anne, and then took a local guide, the journey could be safely made and a night spent at the abbey. It did not house the bones of St Michael, or even one of his feathers, as the credulous believed, but it had something as good: the skull of the blessed St Aubert, who had founded it on the direct orders of the Archangel. At the back, wonderfully worn smooth by generations of reverent fingers, was the hole where St Michael had touched Aubert's head to summon him to the task.[11] There was also the immensely heavy silver reliquary of St Aubert's body, a new relic of St Eustace just presented by Abbot Jolivet, and many other treasures.

All that Sutton could do in his frustration was to stand on the shore at Genêts, and gaze out across the Bay. He could not go on his way wearing a badge of Our Lady of Tombelaine, nor one of St Michael, whether the dramatic one of him killing the dragon of evil or the even more sobering one of him weighing souls; not even the simple pewter cockleshell badge that some pilgrims still preferred, as a symbol of the antiquity of this shrine and their own overcoming of the sea to reach it. Perhaps he did spend a few extra minutes instead looking along the beach until he found a real cockle, which he could drill out and wear around his neck as a personal reminder that he had at least tried to be faithful to the first part of his vow.

Then there was nothing else to be done, the day being not yet over, but to turn away and trudge on, down the coast a little further before nightfall. At least in these parts he could be sure of finding a place to stay. From the priory at St Leonard he had to turn inland, up-river, until he found a bridge at Ponts. From there, the main road south cut through Avranches and on over a bridge close to the mouth of the next river. But in Avranches, with its garrison and royal castle, rumours were circulating of unease to the south. It was better to return to the Ponts Hôtel-Dieu, close under the city walls, and wait for clearer advice in the daylight.

10
Brigands or Bravehearts?

Je suis Francoys, dont ce me poise
Né de Paris emprès Pontoise,
Or d'une corde d'une toise
Saura mon col que mon cul poise.[1]

Avranches was an unhappy island in a troubled sea. Set up on their hill overlooking the bay, its people had not taken kindly to the English conquest. Close to the Breton border and long resigned to border raids, the city had been recaptured briefly by the Armagnacs, only to fall again swiftly to the English. Its loyalties were deeply divided, the bishop overtly hostile, and on all sides there were complaints: at the new taxes, the violence of the outlaws, the burden of the garrison, and the imposition of a new coinage that so pointedly displayed the English leopard in place of the fleur-de-lys.

The physical damage was everywhere evident, and nowhere more clearly than in the cathedral: 'the city itself was very frequently besieged by hostile forces, the monthly income of the aforesaid church and chapter decreased to such an extent that the belltower, walls, and other buildings of the said church and its glass, all of which had been broken, ruined and knocked down in the aforementioned continuing sieges and by the turmoil of such wars, could not be restored, rebuilt or repaired...'[2]

From outside the city, rumours came in of seething discontent. The coastal communities were being squeezed between rapacious requisitioning parties from Mont St Michel and the tightening noose of the English siege. Inland, a broad belt of forest sheltered a volatile mix of impoverished peasants, unpaid and violent ex-mercenaries, and desperate Armagnac soldiers fighting a rearguard action against the new order. The worst of the economic and political chaos of the civil war had subsided, but it takes decades for a society to outgrow its poisonous effects. And now the climate had added a new twist. Two wet summers with dismal harvests had been succeeded in 1422 by a summer so dry that many crops had yielded less than had gone to sow them; then a severe winter had followed, so that the grain reserves were almost all gone and even fodder for horses was in critically short supply.

All these troubles bred unrest like a hot summer breeds plague. But how to distinguish between a genuine grievance and unscrupulous outlawry, between brigandage and enemy action? To try to get on top of the problem, the courts offered a bounty of six French 'Tours' pounds (six weeks' pay for an archer) per person captured alive, if a conviction was secured. 'Brigans, larrons, traitres et agresseurs de chemins'[3] were brought in and tried. Common criminals and brigands were hanged; those who could prove they were politically motivated were granted a swifter death by beheading; soldiers who had not taken the oath of allegiance to King Henry were liberated as prisoners of war, if a ransom could be paid.

The dislocation of life caused by three generations of war ran deep. The rule of law was tenuous at best, and the courts were kept busy with a depressing stream of rapes, murders, arson attacks, burglaries and botched protection rackets. In and among these, there were about a dozen executions for treason, and several of these were men from the cluster of villages just south-west of Avranches.[4] Worryingly for Sutton, that was precisely the district he had to cross next. Moreover, the six parishes that made up the fief of Montaigu, lying right across his road south, had reverted to rebel control in the autumn, and nobody seemed sure where their allegiance now lay. To avoid this area, he would have to make a wide looping diversion to the east, and cross the River Sélune farther upstream. As far as the old pilgrim town of St James he should be able to find his way, but after that he would need a guide.

So he left Avranches heading into the mid-morning sun, not due south as he had hoped. Past the lazar and church of St Quentin with its scallop-decorated cross, the road dropped down to the Sélune at Ducey, amid lush buttercup meadows. There a wooden bridge carried another pilgrim road over the river towards Mont St Michel, close by Montmorel Abbey at the aptly named hamlet of Le Pavement,[5] and there Sutton turned south and followed the byways up the little Beuvron valley, two easy leagues to St James.

A priory, a lazar and an Hôtel-Dieu rubbed shoulders here with the newer reality of an active garrison. First French, then factional Armagnac soldiery, and now the English 'Goddams'[6] were quartered here, each succeeding army imposing its own kind of control on their varied frontiers. For 70 years this had been a district on the edge of chaos, and 40 years ago the wars had come so close to the town that the hospital was virtually destroyed. But St James owed its prosperity to pilgrims and travellers, and making arrangements for accommodating them was a priority. The priory, founded by King William's ancestors before the Conquest, claimed to house a small relic of St James himself[7] and some pilgrims were drawn to this for its own sake. But many more lodged there as they came and went to Mont St Michel and to numerous other shrines, far and near.

Priories and hospices such as those at St James were ideal places for picking up the latest advice for travellers: the state of the roads and relevant political news. With the constant two-way movement of pilgrims, merchants and pedlars, the information was seldom more than one day old. Only one St James man had gone to the gallows for brigandage, in the unquiet year of 1419–20, but in the forests to the west and south the lawlessness persisted. How best to negotiate this barrier, backed as it was by the mighty River Loire? Safe roads were few, and the political situation was far more complex than Sutton had realized before he left home. There were two bridges he could aim for, one at Nantes and one further east at Angers. The road to Nantes would take him down the length of the Breton Marches, by now a traditional region of border incursions, disputes and raids, despite the fact that Brittany and England were supposed to be allies. But the lands to the south-east were still not under English control, still had not submitted to the three-year-old Peace of Troyes. On the whole, the Breton border was the better option, until such time as the Treaty was obeyed. At least Brittany was a virtually independent Duchy, tied as much by obligation to England as by fealty to France, and senior English officers were being employed to adjudicate in the continuing border disputes.

There remained the pressing problem of how to strike west and find a safe road down towards Nantes. Here again the Blessed Virgin was available when Sutton needed help. Prayers to Our Lady of St Martin[8] would produce a reliable guide to show the way on byroads to the neighbouring Benedictine priory of Tremblay, an awkward journey across the grain of the land, avoiding the worst trouble-spots, but easy enough with local knowledge.

PART IV

Brittany – Another Duchy

11
Independent Politics

How many [angels] do you think there are here at this moment? You will reply 'As many as there are persons present', and you will be right, for each one has his guardian angel. But beside these, there are many million others.[1]

Robert Sutton believed implicitly in the power of prayer, and in the presence of angels. He also believed in a titanic universal battle between good and evil, in which there were casualties on both sides. Every church he saw was a well-head of power and a reminder of the immediacy of this conflict, liberally adorned as they were with carvings and paintings of devils, saints and angels.

The Schoolmen may have had their complex hierarchies of heaven, but for the ordinary believer the most accessible and relevant part of the heavenly armies ranged on your side were the four archangels (of whom Michael was paramount for a pilgrim), and the innumerable guardian angels, whose activities blended with those of the patron saints. The distinction, indeed, was so blurred that it was generally believed that Michael was a saint as well as an archangel, and many thought he had left not only some of his feathers here on earth but his footprints too. The ubiquity of the angels underpinned the imperative of Christian hospitality: 'Be not forgetful to entertain strangers: for thereby some have entertained angels unawares.'[2]

His road from Normandy made smoother by his guides, Sutton pushed on south the next morning, on the long haul to Rennes. At first he travelled up the Couesnon valley, through an open and pleasantly undulating landscape dotted with villages and towns. But gradually the trees closed in and he entered the Forest of Rennes, where the road became many forked, slippery with grey clay and uncomfortably hemmed in by dripping trees. Squirrels crashing in the branches, and blackbirds scuffling in the undergrowth, both have the power to terrify, in woods known to be haunted by brigands and devils. An anxious afternoon hurrying along, reciting *Aves* and *Pater Nosters*, ended with the unexpected but most welcome sight of a large Cistercian abbey in a gentle valley clearing. The double monastery of St Sulpice of Notre Dame du Nid au Merle,[3] presided over by a lady abbess, had recovered somewhat from the terrible pounding it had taken in the wars 70 years earlier, and was open for business. Set on his way on the high road to Rennes the next morning, Sutton could afford to take a lighter view of the noises in the woods.

The young Duke of Brittany had now declared himself to be firmly in the English camp, but in the years in which he had been wavering, many disaffected Normans had fled to his territories, joining the hundreds of refugees coming into the cities from the devastated countryside round about. As a result, Rennes was not merely bursting at the seams, it had spilled over into rapidly growing suburbs to the east and south, and was humming with activity. A wooden palisade had just been put up, enclosing an area three times the size of the old city, and work was beginning on its conversion to more permanent walls.

Sutton came in past the Dominican convent, its church newly completed but the conventual buildings barely begun, and entered the Ville Neuve district through a temporary gate that led directly to the Franciscan-controlled Hôtel-Dieu. Once outside the city walls but now within the palisade, it was rapidly becoming engulfed in a tide of new streets and houses. This Hôtel-Dieu of St James was the proper place for pilgrims, in a city well provided with foundations for the care of all conditions and needs. The hospitals of St Anne and St Yves took in the sick and some wayfarers; a new hospital of St Marguerite, founded in 1412, cared particularly for poor travellers, and there were also the guest houses of the many religious houses, including the Abbey of St George in the eastern suburbs.[4]

This ninth of May was a doubly important day for Sutton, and a suitable one for a half-day rest. It was the Sunday before Rogationtide, a three-day period of fasting and prayer for the coming harvest of fields, orchards and gardens, and it was also the Feast of the Translation of St Andrew. Back home in Worcester, and wherever there were churches dedicated in his honour, the day would be marked with particular care. Here in Rennes, it was only accorded the status of a minor festival, with a special celebration of Mass. The harvest was of much wider concern, especially in this spring of shortages, and the outdoor processions to bless the crops over the next three days, with the priests in penitential purple vestments and the bells of the city tolling, would no doubt be especially well observed. Meanwhile, the narrow and twisting alleys of old Rennes offered a choice of churches to attend.[5] The cathedral of St Pierre, over by the monumental western Mordelaise Gate, was at the heart of city life, and two blocks away the parish church of St Sauveur was home to its patroness, Notre Dame des Miracles. She had intervened decisively to save Rennes from destruction in the wars two generations earlier, and was active still. And St George's Abbey, once outside the city and now in its new eastward extension, owned an object of great importance for any Englishman: '… in the sacristy they show St George's entire leg and many other marvels.'[6]

Fortified by this sight and by a half-day's rest, Sutton could set off on the Monday morning conscious that he was now in a relatively untroubled landscape, where no major conflicts had been waged for 40 years. He could even consider continuing his journey towards the Loire in the company of some of the numerous merchants and other regular travellers who passed between the ducal seats of Rennes and Nantes, if he could find a group whom he felt he could trust. Such men knew 'the most sure ways from town to town: of the which there have been often divers, and one better than the other, because of war and other misdoers for the time'.[7] They travelled on horseback, but their pack animals and attendants kept them down to a pace that a fit walker could sustain without much difficulty.

From Rennes to Bain-de-Bretagne, Mouais, Nozay and Héric, the merchants not only knew the best roads, they knew where reliable lodgings were to be found. La Croix Verte in Bain was solidly respectable. Grand-Fougeray, despite its attractions as a large town with many facilities, was to be avoided because that route led one too far west into the forests of the Marches. Instead, at Mouais Sutton could stay at the little priory with its tiny old church, and hear a Mass for St Pancras next morning before rejoining the cavalcade to Nozay and the slate-grey Priory of St Saturnin. The merchants might elect to stay in an inn, but pilgrims preferred a religious house, however small, particularly on the eve of such an important festival as Ascension. The feast day would begin with the solemn extinguishing of the Easter Candle after the Gospel at morning Mass; the full drama of the Ascension, with the lifting up of the Risen Christ until he vanished through the trap-door in the church ceiling,[8] would be enacted in churches all across Christendom later on in the day.

Inns were all very well as a fall-back, offering suitable food for fast and feast days as required, and despite the dominance of Breton there was usually someone available who spoke some French. If not, the bilingual merchants were able to translate. But everything at an inn had to be paid for, separately itemized, and here was a problem. The newly minted Anglo-French salut was treated with suspicion, English pennies were not at parity with Breton money, and Sutton had none of that to offer. Each night he would have to pay in coin for bed, candles, wine, bread, beans, cheese or fish and any extras that the landlord managed to throw in. Prices varied alarmingly, and the complexity of the system of coinage and its relationship to any notional purchasing power was so fluid as to make the whole business of paying for goods fraught with difficulty. English, Breton, Anglo-Norman and Burgundian coins were all circulating legally, many of them in very debased metal. A salut, one might learn, was equivalent to an écu, and worth half an English noble which was valued at one mark.[9] But a French 'franc' in early 1420 had been worth 16 Parisian sols, while later the same year an écu worth 18 sols was equivalent to four francs. The situation was further complicated by the rebel Armagnacs using the currency as an offensive weapon, minting and circulating counterfeit money, nearly black in colour because it was so debased, causing a complete loss of confidence in any dark-coloured coins. No wonder, then, if Sutton preferred priories and hospitals where possible, where he could attend divine service and where he could make an offering in good English silver pennies and halfpennies, confident that even if his hosts were unable to use it as coin, it could be melted down or sold for its value as metal.

From the merchants, Sutton might pick up something of the political situation: the recent meeting at Arras far off in Artois, at which the English Regent, the Duke of Bedford, had conferred with the Dukes of Burgundy and Brittany and sealed their mutual compact against the Armagnacs with marriage alliances; the news that the so-called dauphin was missing, presumed dead, after an accident at La Rochelle; and the old civil war between rival branches of the Breton ducal family that was in danger of flaring up again with the added dimension of a power struggle within the ruling de Montforts, some siding with the English and some serving openly in the Armagnac army. And from merchants and monks alike he would have learnt of the recent death of a man already revered as a saint: Vincent Ferrer, whose last great preaching tours had taken him around this very part of Brittany, to Nantes, Rennes and Vannes where he had finally died in April 1419 and where miracles were already happening at his tomb. He had encouraged and advised the Duchess in her childlessness, and his simple prescription of a twice-daily recital of the *Pater Noster, Ave, Credo* and a Psalm had procured the desired son not just for the ducal couple but for many other disciples as well. His practical advice comforted people in fear of devils and tempests, requiring them to concentrate on repeating the *Credo* and crossing themselves at each article, and he had recommended frequent use of a simple prayer to the angels for daily support:

> *O Angel of God, whom God hath appointed to be my guardian,*
> *enlighten and protect me, direct and govern me. Amen.*[10]

12
Over the Loire

Item this town of Nantis lies between two swift rivers, the one called the Lier. Where we entered it divides itself into six arms, over each of which is a wooden bridge. In between there is also a stone bridge which crosses an evil marsh, 450 paces long . . . In this church lie many holy bodies, the names of which were unknown to us.[1]

Where the Rivers Erdre and Sèvre came into the Loire, a chaplet of islands and sandbanks supported the Seven Bridges of Nantes. Twelve leagues inland from the sea, it was the lowest bridging point by far, a crossroads, meeting place and entrepôt. Episcopal see, ducal capital and cosmopolitan port, it was a city determinedly independent of France and devoted to raffish bad behaviour. Its Mardis Gras festival was dedicated to the spurious but much admired 'St Dégobillard',[2] in whose honour the people yearly celebrated their last day of licence before Lent began.

This paradoxical city of Nantes stood within walls so extensive that even the convents of the Carmelites, Franciscans and Dominicans were all inside, with open gardens and orchards to spare. Three times the size of Rennes, four times the population of Worcester, it had an elegant aristocratic centre. But in the butchers' quarter where the road came in over the River Erdre from the north, and down in the closely packed alleys near the quays, the filth was legendary. In heavy rain it used to wash sluggishly down the streets and block the city gates so they had to be dug open.

Three things had shaken Nantes recently: two dreadful fires in 1405 and 1415, and a visit from Vincent Ferrer, who had preached in the city for 12 days in March 1417, performing miracles and convincing many of the need for repentance. People had gathered in their hundreds to hear him, heedless of the rain and snow, and had then set about rebuilding their churches, their homes and, in some cases at least, their godliness. The cathedral tower had collapsed in the second fire and was newly rebuilt; the nave was still in urgent need of repair, but the old ambulatory around the crypt had survived. There the martyrs and saints of Nantes were interred, St Gohard and the city patrons Donatien and Rogatien, whose feast-day fair took place on 2 May.

Other construction work was going on too. The Dominicans had moved to a better site and had consecrated their new church; now they were busy with the conventual buildings. The Carmelites, in the centre of the city just to the left of the main north–south thoroughfare, had managed to gain ducal patronage. A timely miracle at their house in 1365 had given them new prominence, and when released from his recent captivity in the Breton civil war, the present Duke had made them an extraordinary gift of his own weight in gold. With a shrewd eye for long-term profits, this was being invested in houses and vacant plots throughout the city. Many of the parish churches and chapels were also being repaired, while out on the first island, La Saulzaie, a new suburb was rapidly developing around the scatter of older houses.

The bridges themselves were constantly needing attention. Every winter the floods and frosts took their toll and then the spring melt waters hurled themselves and their burden of tree trunks and stones at the piles, further weakening them. The damage was so regular, and the traffic so vital, that a permanent team of workmen was employed to maintain the bridges and causeways, and to operate a ferry service when necessary.

Six of the bridges were wooden, the seventh made of stone, but all were paved, as were the main streets through the city. Most of the islands were inhabited, in spite of periodic floods, and La Saulzaie Island was famous for its numerous inns and taverns. Farther out, Toussaints Island had a priory, a recently opened lay music and grammar school and an almonry of St Jacques Pèlerin which took in and helped pilgrims and travellers. The standard two nights' lodging given to pilgrims would give Sutton a much-needed day in a town big enough to supply his wants: a cobbler to repair his boots, a money-changer to provide some coin he could be confident of using in the

Armagnac-held territories farther south, and information and advice about the best route to take from here.

A cobbler was easy to find in a city the size of Nantes, with a huge butchers' quarter and a large population of all ranks to cater for. Leaving the boots while they were re-soled was less straightforward, involving a filthy barefoot walk through the unmentionable muck of the streets. If the brothers of Toussaints Priory observed the traditional ritual of footwashing for their guests, it can seldom have been more welcome, especially if they also lent him shoes from their almonry supplies when he returned to the cobbler to reclaim his own.

Money was also something Nantes dealt in habitually. It had its own mint, and being so close to the borders of Poitou and Anjou, as well as a port, it was accustomed to handling foreign coin. The Jews had all gone long since, as they had from England, and it was the Italian bankers who were beginning to get a toe-hold in the city finances. With their complex accounting methods, their houses springing up in every trading centre of Europe and their excellent and very safe bills of exchange, they were the future of international transactions. Meanwhile there was a great variety of coinage to be seen, reflecting Nantes' international trade. The city's two quay areas could only handle small vessels, but from the busily shuttling barges came a surprising range of goods: Breton salt being trans-shipped to go on upstream; English lead; Spanish wine, fruit and iron; French wine; and above all wool and cloth, from England, Flanders and Germany. All of this involved financial deals, some of it with direct payments, and it also brought into the city sailors and merchants with outlandish foreign coins in their pockets, from every nation of Christendom and many mysterious distant places too. Equipped with pocket books, tables and scales, the money-changers sifted good coin from counterfeit, pure metal from alloy, and did a roaring trade. English coin was always in demand, for its stability and purity, and changing it was easy. What mattered more was keeping one's reserves hidden, only revealing the small sum to be exchanged, for a full money bag certainly invited theft and murder in unfamiliar alleyways, regardless of the pilgrim habit worn.

Advice was readily come by, but interpreting it without the benefit of local knowledge was harder, especially as it came mostly through Sutton's imperfect French, his even more sketchy Latin, or his informants' attempts at English. At least Bishop Jean de Malestroit of Nantes was pro-English, as well as intent on fostering better relations between Duke and Church. So any Englishmen in the city could move around and mix freely, and exchange news. It seemed that Charles, the erstwhile dauphin, was still alive, having survived the accident in La Rochelle, but he had withdrawn to the east, into the pro-Armagnac rebel heartlands around Bourges. The English and Burgundians had taken to deriding him as 'King of Bourges', since that was apparently the extent of his ambitions.

A more immediate concern for now was the direction to take next, once over the Loire. The road south crossed the Vendée hills, the heartland of Gilles de Rais, the young Lord of Tiffauges, Pouzauges and Machecoul. He was an ardent protagonist of Charles, and was known to be an impetuous and rather ruthless soldier, with a large private retinue. Could he and his henchmen be trusted to let an English pilgrim pass unmolested?[3] Then, beyond the Vendée, an area of low-lying land that had been carefully drained and maintained by the five abbeys that lived off its richness, had returned to unproductive marsh during the wars, and was now described as an impassable and ague-ridden waste. Even if Sutton did take the hill roads south, he would be forced to divert east towards Niort to find a way around the head of the swamps.

So the safest option seemed to be to head south-east and follow up the Sèvre valley until a road south presented itself, aiming roughly for Niort and trusting to St Michael, St James and his guardian angels to show the way.

The first two nights beyond Nantes, certainly, would be under the personal aegis of St James, at the Pirmil hospice on the south bank of the Loire and then at the St Jacques priory at Clisson. Half-an-hour's walk beyond the main Poissonnerie Gate of Nantes, over the bridges, through the crowds thronging the causeways of the island suburbs, was a fort guarding the southern approaches to the city. There the Benedictines of St Jacques of Pirmil had been lodging pilgrims coming and going to Nantes for 250 years. Thence, the road to Clisson and the border ran past a line of five priories, at Vertou, St Fiacre, Monnieres, Gorges and Clisson St Jacques. It was an

unusually well-provided road, with a guest house never more than
an hour away.

Mid-May was not yet summer, but on this pleasant road the sun
was now noticeably warm on the cheeks, and after the damp of
England and all the reminders of a hard winter just past, the bursting
tendrils of the vines were a pleasant and novel sight. Between Vertou
and St Fiacre, a ferry took travellers over the River Sèvre, gentle at
this point in its meanderings. In another month, it would be fordable
here, but for now foot passengers, horsemen and carts alike had to
rely on the ferry, or take the longer road to the north.

Up on its ridge between two rivers, St Fiacre Priory afforded a
salutary reminder of life's complexities. Fiacre, Irish hermit-exile,
misogynist vegetable-grower, showed many faces to the world in his
adopted France, not least his patronage of victims of venereal disease,
and his notoriously hasty temper. Henry V had incurred his wrath,
pious King Henry who carried a portion of the True Cross everywhere
with him in his baggage train, for expressing a wish to translate one of
Fiacre's relics from Meaux. Some said the dying King had been
tormented by visions of the unquiet saint. Some muttered that Henry's
lingering and unexplained death was the Curse of St Fiacre. Here, at his
priory, Sutton was impelled to kneel before the spade-wielding statue
of the acerbic saint and pray earnestly for the soul of the King.

The complex loyalties of the Clisson family, too, might touch a
traveller. Like innumerable families all over Europe, considerations
of local politics weighed more with them than international
obligations. Old Lord Olivier de Clisson had changed sides like a
roast on a spit, but shortly before his death he had settled firmly in
the Breton ducal camp. His daughter Margot, not to be outdone in
family opportunism, took the opposite view in nearly everything,
and had almost brought off a spectacular coup, imprisoning the
Duke in her castle. But Duke John now being restored, the Clisson
family were in eclipse and their great castle had been entrusted to
the Duke's brother, who had promptly declared for the Armagnacs.

Yet again the unanswerable question: was an Englishman with a
purse of silver a legitimate target for an Armagnac lord, or did his
pilgrim status confer some sort of immunity? Better not to find out,
but to stay with the Benedictines at the priory by the St Jacques gate,

and slip through the town in the early hours, down the steep alleyways and stepped lanes to the wooden bridge over the gorge-like River Sèvre.[4] Beyond, in the suburb of La Trinité, the Benedictine nuns continued their custom of handing out regular doles of bread and money to the destitute, while nearby a convent of reformed Observant Franciscans was being built, paid for by Margot de Clisson according to the terms of her father's will.

Old Lord Olivier had been a legend in his time, but as Sutton was uncomfortably aware, he was now entering a land where legend and fact were inextricably mixed, where serpents married men and where dragons flew. A land where, contrary to what he had been told at home, the writ of England did not run and chaos was king.

PART V

Armagnac France

13
Through the Lands of Melusine

It is seen often when a man hath yssued out of hys countree and hath seen many awounder and mervayllous thynges whiche he never wold have byleved hit by here sayeng, without he had hadd the sight of hit.[1]

Somewhere east of Clisson, Robert Sutton passed into rebel lands. Not that it made any immediate impact on the lives of travellers; no river or dyke or even a particular range of hills could be said to define the border, no twin garrisons glowered at each other across the divide. It was a fluid division, existing in the minds of the great lords, but scarcely impinging on the lives of the masses, whose allegiance in so far as they felt one was to Brittany, Poitou or Anjou, not to Armagnac or Burgundian, France or England.

There were more travellers on the road now, as the weather slowly improved, and at Mortagne-sur-Sèvre, Sutton found Benedictines who treated pilgrims just the same, regardless of their origins. A 50-year English occupation had ended a full generation ago, the castle had changed hands yet again, and now the priory church was newly repaired. A long tradition of pilgrim traffic on the way to St Hilary at Poitiers made Mortagne a prosperous house, with a famous relic of St Léger deposited there for safe keeping way back in some other far-off wars. Poitiers was too far into rebel territory to tempt Sutton, and in any case would involve a big detour, but here at Mortagne there was a shrine of the Virgin, a beautiful Lady blackened with the smoke of ten thousand flames of devotion, whose tender and unsearchable smile of treasured knowledge was worth all his trouble to reach her.

The Blessed Virgin, under whatever epithet he found her, was a tower of strength and comfort in increasingly foreign lands. The helpful brothers directed him to his next stop, six leagues further up the valley, where the Sèvre was reduced to a gentle flow in warm soft meadows set in pleasant hills. This was Clisson family land again, the newly built manor at La Deffend proclaiming an enclave of loyalty in a world of strangers. Soon after passing it, he came to the sanctuary of Beauchêne. The precious statue of the Virgin, once lost as the monks fled a Viking raid, had been joyfully rediscovered safely hidden in the hollow trunk of an ancient oak, and set in a place of honour in her church. To her, the old Seigneur had presented a pillow from Judaea, which was said to have belonged to the Holy Family in Nazareth. The young Seigneur, his son, was still restoring the chapel for her, embellishing the chancel and adding a complete set of new windows.

Despite the sympathetic understanding of many, each day now made Sutton more acutely aware of a language barrier. The northern-style French that he was familiar with, knowing more or less 'how to speak and pronounce well, and to write correctly sweet French, which is the finest and most graceful language, the noblest to speak of any in the world after Latin of the schools',[2] no longer seemed to serve him in rural Poitou. Whether through genuine incomprehension, or deliberate obtuseness, people more and more often stared at him in blank perplexity, or gave random and unintelligible replies. Several times, when he was sure he had understood what was said, he suspected later that he had been deliberately misled. Their accents were strange, and their garbled speech was peppered with unfamiliar words.

In the religious houses where he spent these nights, frequent dealings with travellers encouraged a less parochial view and communication was much easier; for most of his needs he could in any case still fall back on his rudimentary Latin. In one of these houses, he finally obtained definite news of the Armagnac position. Charles, known in these parts as the Dauphin, had indeed gone to La Rochelle in the previous autumn, to test the loyalty of the city which was his only link with the sea and his Scottish allies. But uncertain of the extent of his support, he had travelled without pomp, and once west of Poitiers had kept to the byroads. La Rochelle had indeed been wavering in its allegiance, with a Breton governor who might have soon declared for the English alliance. If he had done so, the city could have controlled access to Poitou and squeezed the Dauphin's supply lines; hostile to England, it made a nest of pirates that exposed the soft underbelly of Brittany and her sea routes to Bordeaux.

Arriving in La Rochelle in mid-October 1422, Charles had found the city in a state of considerable alarm, fearing attack from both sides and prey to conflicting rumours. Acting with unusual decision, he had immediately called a council meeting for the following day, to assemble at his lodgings at the bishop's palace. There, so many people had crammed into the audience chamber that the floor had collapsed and the entire crowd crashed through the room below and into the basement, with many casualties. In the uproar, cries of treason were soon heard and rioting erupted in the streets. It had taken four days to restore order. Meanwhile, it had been discovered that Charles had most providentially escaped death, because he had been seated at the end of the room built onto the old city wall, and the great thickness of the masonry, combined with the stoutness of his chair (in which he had descended through the rubble), had broken his fall. On the fourth day, a second meeting had been convened and the surviving members of the council, much shaken, had sworn a solemn oath to Charles as Regent of France during his father's insanity, in defiance of the Treaty of Troyes. When he left the city the next day, injured but able to travel, Charles had taken with him the piece of stone that had hit him on the head. Attributing his miraculous escape to the intervention of St Michael, he had sent the stone and a crystal bust of himself to Mont St Michel, with an offering for a votive mass.[3]

So Sutton now knew for certain that the Dauphin was still alive, and some cities at least were prepared to acknowledge him as such. Or, now his father was dead, to go further and style him King Charles VII, despite the legal title of Henry VI to the Crowns of both England and France under the regency of his uncle John of Bedford. This meant that through Poitou Sutton must continue to try to find religious houses where he could stay each night, and not trust to inns, with uncertain loyalties and an increasing problem communicating even his most basic needs. He also had a third worry playing on his mind: a worry he might have scoffed at safe at home, but which here, alone except for chance encounters with men who might equally well be friend or foe, alone and often lost in a well-wooded and poorly maintained landscape, seemed too tangible for comfort. For this Poitou, as every well-read European knew, was a land of serpents and dragons.

These monsters crawled over every church door. They twined round pillars and glared from frescoes. They symbolized temptation, lust and the chaos that accompanies sin, as Sutton knew to his cost. Give way, and order breaks down and mankind becomes a changeling, unstable in form, half-human half-beast, careering down towards the freakish disorder of hell. Mad monstrosities ate away at the capitals, tore at domestic animals and foliage and feasted on condemned souls. Terrifying reminders of the gossamer-fine boundary between heaven and hell, order and chaos, normality and nightmare. Every step through Poitou took Sutton closer to the great arc of forests that lay somewhere ahead, where beasts of all kinds were rumoured to lurk, while every sunny rock already seemed to flicker with the departure of a basking lizard, dragon's kith.

Dragons there certainly were, and many other monsters too. John Mandeville had written of lions, unicorns, white elephants with noses like arms, and the basilisk that killed you with its stare.[4] Unicorns were known from their horns, occasionally sold on from eastern merchants; dragons, though seemingly expelled from Christendom by the saints of old, lived on in remote places. Dragon's blood, crimson and resinous, was still available in tiny amounts and at high prices, and was a potent weapon in the apothecaries' armoury, against burns and the bloody flux.[5]

But here in Poitou the banished beasts had returned and the nightmare had stepped into the light of day, just a few hundred years ago. Poitou, the borderland of France, where the battles of Charlemagne and the Black Prince were as close to the imagination as the present wars, was the Land of Melusine. Her story, the tragedy of the changeling serpent-Countess of Lusignan, was told and retold from parent to wide-eyed child, and now Jean d'Arras had collected

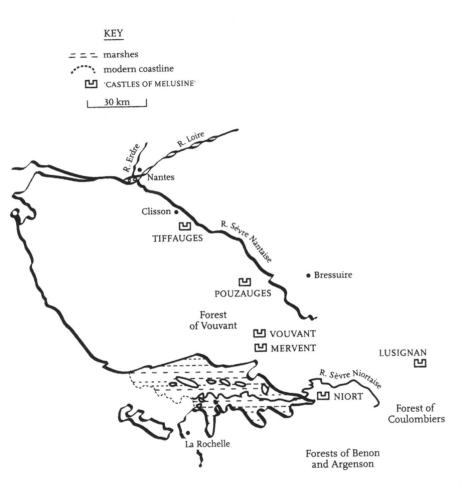

The lands of Melusine

together all the tales and written them in a book so popular it could be read in any city in Europe. 'And semblable wyse this historye is more credible for as moche as it is not auctorised by one man only, but also by many noble Clerkes.'[6]

Melusine, the lovely fairy, was doomed to change her form every Saturday, 'fro the navel dounward in lykness of a grete serpent, the tayll as grete and thykk as a barell'. Against her better judgement, she became the bride of Count Raymondyn, but was betrayed by her brother-in-law and so the couple were forced to part. At their final terrible leave-taking, Melusine leapt out of an upper window and 'she toke her way to Lusynen, makyng in thayer [the air] by her furyousnes suche horryble crye and noyse that it semed al thayer to be replete with thundre and tempeste'.[7] Count Raymondyn, equally broken-hearted, never saw his wife again, although she haunted the surrounding forests for many years and her body has never been found. But she left her land a proud legacy, in her descendants the Lusignan family and in a series of dramatic castles, each built in a single night and sustained by her magic: Vouvant, Mervent, Niort, Lusignan, Pouzauges and Tiffauges. Through the lands ringed by these castles, through hills and forests where Raymondyn had hunted and Melusine might still appear, Sutton now had to find his way.

14
Marshes, Monks and Marauders

…holy freres,
That serchen every lond and every streem,
As thikke as motes in the sonne-beem.[1]

At least Poitou offered a good choice of religious houses, with commanderies, convents, priories and the occasional abbey, of every conceivable size and Order. The Knights Templar had run more houses here than in the whole of England, and when they were disbanded their entire landholding had been transferred to the Hospitallers, the Knights of St John. So Hospitaller priories and commanderies, mostly with only a prior and one or two brothers, dotted the landscape, farming, sending surplus revenue to their headquarters, but also offering hospitality and nursing care to pilgrims. With the exception of the big commanderies and regional headquarters, the Hospitallers were a rural phenomenon, based in tiny hamlets that had often grown up around the original Templar base. Not surprising then that they were popular with pilgrims, so often struggling to reach a distant town before dark and relieved to catch sight of the familiar black robes and the Hospitallers' eight-pointed cross, which promised a refuge for the night.

Mendicants of all kinds were also numerous and well loved in Poitou, but unlike the Hospitallers they were mainly based in towns. Much more so than in England, these friars were a mainstay of popular religion, and coexisted relatively peacefully with the other Orders. In England, tensions were always there, seldom far below the surface: jealousy, bigotry, and accusations of hypocrisy, idleness or greed. The Sack Friars had once had several convents here, but they were gone now, just as they were from England, legislated out of existence in the general tidying up of the Mendicant Orders. Here in Poitou, the Franciscans had seized the opportunity and expanded to take their place. At first, the Regular Franciscans opened new houses or took over and developed abandoned Sack Friar property, to meet the pastoral need created, but in the last few decades the Observant Franciscans had reached France, opening convent after convent in a wave of reforming enthusiasm. One such was the new establishment at Clisson, and another opened almost simultaneously at Bressuire.[2]

The Bressuire house, founded in a town that already had four priories and an almonry, was a success from the start. Situated within the walls, up on the crag near the huge castle, it was blessed with a papal embassy and seigneurial support for its godparents. A rich citizen named Jean de Chiché donated one house in the town, the Seigneur Jean de Beaumont purchased and then donated the plot adjacent, and the Observants began building their convent in June 1405. From an initial brotherhood of five, the house quickly grew in size and influence, the friars being noted for their hard work and zeal, especially in preaching and pastoral work among the populace.[3]

Entering Bressuire from the west, the town was an impressive sight, its castle walls rising up from the golden crag above the Dolo River. Spread at its feet, the two priories of St Cyprien and De La Tousche Chevrier counterbalanced the series of mills and tannery works along the riverside and told of a secure and prosperous town. Out to the south, the Almonry St Jacques spread its protective wings over travellers in need.

Another day south, another day of warm sunshine and gentle hills, another day with St James, ended at Hérisson, with its church and inn of St George. How comforting to find the dragon-slaying saint of England in Poitou. Hérisson, a crossroads and halting place on the old salt road into central France, was rebuilding its priory of St Jean, in strong grey granite. The archivolt of the tower door was newly engraved '1422' in acknowledgement of a phase of work completed.

On again, past the priory of St Eulalie at Secondigny, dedicated to the virgin martyr of Spain so dearly loved in France. Then, in an area of heath among the richer arable land, the Antonine hospital of St Marc La Lande. These, like the lazars before them, were a response to a desperate medical and spiritual need. They would take in all travellers, of course, but their especial vocation was in their hospitals for the victims of St Antony's fire, a terrifying disease that knew no bounds. In extreme cases, sufferers went mad with the pain, while their limbs rotted away from the living body. In the hospitals, the Antonines prepared these unfortunates for their end with meditations on the Passion, and eased their agony with poppies, hemlock and warm red wine.[4] Milder cases did recover, helped it was thought by doses of woad and by owning one of the Antonines' characteristic bells which they used when asking for alms for their charitable work. In their black robes and wearing their distinctive blue T-shaped 'Tau' cross, the Antonines were a focus of frenzied devotion in years when the 'fire' struck.[5]

The previous year having been so dry, the hospital had no patients with the fire, and Sutton could obtain first-class medical attention for his own relatively trifling needs. More ointment for his feet first of all, rubbed sore again by new boot soles, the last of the spring's scented violets to help clear the lice from his garments, and tansy leaves against the fleas. The only thing the Antonines could not offer him was a solid meat meal, for he had reached the eve of Pentecost. But such an affluent house would feed him well, on fine wheat bread, and potage or fish, and their own good wine, and would give him a better bed than many. And before he left the next day, he walked barefoot for a moment in the miraculous healing Pentecost dew, and then went to the church and Mass.

The '*Veni, Creator Spiritus*'[6] took him straight back to the many Pentecosts he had witnessed and loved at home, the haunting music at once humbling and serene. But here there was an unexpected extra. As the great blue disc with the painted dove that represented the Spirit was lowered slowly towards the ground, a shower of red rose petals cascaded down, as tongues of fire descending on the waiting people. The judgement of fire perhaps, but also its purifying and its bright hope.

It was not easy to leave the Antonines of St Marc, at the beginning of their celebrations of Pentecost. This was a safe haven, familiar enough to feel a little like home. The Poitou parish clergy, in contrast to these devoted monks, seemed aimless and inept. No wars had touched this area for 50 years, but little had been done to repair the damage. Even a casual observer like Sutton could see the broken-down buildings, the poverty, the lack of pastoral oversight. The bishops of Maillezais and Luçon had both left their sees as their derelict lands returned to marsh and mass emigration crippled the Poitevin economy. In the general collapse of the ecclesiastical superstructure, the parish priests had felt the pinch as much as anyone. With no visitations and little control, the downward spiral was swift. No man of education or culture would endure these conditions, so the rural clergy were chips off the same rude block as their parishioners, illiterate and unversed in the barest essentials of the faith. The people were ignorant of the Creed and Commandments, and their priests seemed incapable of following a suitable moral code.[7]

Out to the west a little way, the five great abbeys of the Marshes were in an especially parlous state. Originally built on islands in a shallow bay, over the years their monks had canalized the rivers, drained and controlled the waters of the bay, and created a rich and fertile plain, producing fine wheat and beans, lush pasture and good wine. But the irrigation system was complex and labour intensive, and the abbeys made natural targets in time of war. Repeatedly pillaged, vandalized and desecrated, many of the buildings were abandoned and their monks joined the general exodus from the land. Those who remained were unable to maintain the canals, and after a few wet winters the work of generations was undone. Impoverished villages clung to low islands in a muddy, fever-ridden swamp, too shallow to navigate but too deep to ford, through which rivers meandered sluggishly towards the sea. The three ancient routes across the bay were largely disused, the ferries unworkable and the roads unsafe, their owners demanding such exorbitant tolls that people avoided using them. Even quite short journeys in this once orderly land became impossible, and the remaining tatters of social cohesion broke down. In December 1419, the prior of Vix explained that his people could not get to Fontenay, two leagues away, 'by reason of the great floods of winter around the said place, situated by the edge of the sea and entirely surrounded by water'.[8]

Some of the monks who remained were drawn into the companies of outlaws and mercenaries who still lived off the land. Abandoned buildings were fortified, or entire priories turned to banditry to survive. The most notorious case was the Hospitaller commandery of Courant, just south of Niort. An enquiry revealed that the church had been thoroughly fortified, and the elderly commander, Guillaume Mercier, together with a Hospitaller priest, a sergeant and a group of their cronies, had organized lightning attacks on any who passed unsuspectingly along the road. This surely was a world gone mad, when priests and brothers became brigands, and the very people one looked to for moral guidance and help were exposed as deep-dyed sinners and criminals.

Sutton had done well to avoid the route that led to the Marshes, but a basic dilemma remained. In these unsettled regions, should he travel by the highways, or byways? On the main roads, there was more war damage, more likelihood of organized ambush, assault and official interference, but perhaps a corresponding safety in numbers. On smaller roads, he might slip by unmolested, but he would be more conspicuous, risking the attentions of outlaws. There would also inevitably be more time wasted getting lost, and fewer people who could show him the way. Fortunately for him, only one day remained before Niort, the first city where he could reasonably expect to meet other long-distance pilgrims, people whom he might be able to trust to share his journey.

As a free port, Niort had once had a stranglehold on the lucrative river-borne trade through the Marshes. As a result, it had initially suffered badly from the wars, but then it had come under the control of the Duke of Berry, uncle of King Charles VI, who had set about restoring its fortunes. Tax revenues were allocated to the corporation for several years for essential repairs, and the Duke built a new quay and harbour, dredged the river channels, defended the city against the toll demands of settlements downstream, rebuilt the main market hall,[9] and generally restored confidence. When the Duke died in 1416 he was sincerely mourned, the more so as he was replaced by a coterie of Armagnacs who began milking the city revenues for their own gain.

Evidence of the restored prosperity and status of Niort was everywhere to be seen. The city Aumonerie by the north gate already had a long tradition of caring for sick residents. In the tangle of streets in the old centre, beyond the parish church of St Andrew, the brand-new market hall stood, eerily cavernous and still on this Pentecost evening but ready to spring into vibrant life when the Feast was over. The city was linked to the new harbour by two fine stone bridges, and mills all up and down the riverbanks, idling for now, would soon be humming with activity again like a hive of sun-wakened bees. Niort was a manufacturing town as well as a market, specializing in chamoiserie, the production of the finest supple gloves by a complicated and infinitely smelly process of tanning in Biscay fish- and whale-oil. The oil, and the pumice blocks that the glovers used for softening the leather, added their own exotic touch to the riverside scene.

In the southern part of the city, beyond the castle (had it really been built by Melusine, or by the scarcely less legendary Queen Eleanor, mother of Coeur de Lion?), broad streets lined with inns led to the St Jean gate, and beyond it to the Almonry St Jacques.[10] Built specifically for Compostelan pilgrims, and with its own cemetery for those who could go no further, the almonry and hospice were a clear indication that here Sutton's pilgrimage entered a new phase.

15
The Holy Heads of St John

He that semeth the wiseste, by jhesus!
Is moost fool, whan it cometh to the preef;
And he that semeth trewest is the theef.[1]

By the time he reached Niort, Sutton had been travelling on his own for seven weeks. There had no doubt been casual aquaintances made along the way, conversations and shared meals, but he had been travelling alone. For a man used to the crowded intimacy of a medieval city and the constant human exchanges of a large household, it was a formidable achievement. The aching loneliness, the friendless tedium, must often have tested him sorely. Telling his beads, counting his paces to the next stream, letting his mind trail off dangerously towards indifference, somehow he had to complete each day. He had little choice in the matter. Once he had undertaken to set off from Worcester alone, once that was incorporated in the pattern of his pilgrimage (to go overland, alone, on foot), it was just not safe to take up with strangers casually met along the way. Everywhere, but especially in France, the roads were channels of fraud and deception. A pedlar might be simply trying to sell ribbons and laces, but how could one be sure? A travelling quack was perhaps only hawking dubious charms and potions, but he might easily be a cover for more sinister operations. And unless one knew the locality and its people, it was impossible to distinguish between a friar on his lawful regular rounds and a wastrel vagabond in a convincing disguise, living off the credulity of the pious.

Behind these suspect individuals lay an underground criminal brotherhood, all the more terrible to pilgrims since they took their title from a mockery of St James: the *Coquillards*. A loosely knit network of gangs, many thousand strong, with their own secret codes and rituals, they were particularly active in north-eastern France, where the collapse of the social order was most complete, but they did not scruple to operate wherever the pickings were rich. Many a pilgrim, befriended on the road, awoke from a drug-induced sleep to find his last sous stolen and his feet bare; many never woke at all.

> *It is also a fact, as is affirmed, that some of the said Coquillards are pick-locks of coffers, chests and treasuries. Others cheat in the changing of gold or buying of goods. Others make, carry and sell false ingots of gold and false gold chains; others carry and sell false jewels in place of diamonds, rubies and other precious stones. Others lie at an inn with some merchant and rob both him and themselves, passing the booty to a member of the band and then lodging a complaint together with the said merchant. Others play with loaded dice and win all the money of those who play with them. Others practise such skilful tricks at card games that none can win money off them. And, what is worse, most of them are footpads and bandits on the highways, robbers and assassins, and it is presumed that it is this which enables them to lead such a dissolute life.*[2]

Ever since leaving home, Sutton had been aware of these risks, more acutely so as he penetrated each day further into Armagnac France. He travelled alone because it was the lesser of two evils, and when he had accepted occasional companionship by day, he had usually shed it again as soon as he could. Even merchants, apparently known and respected on the road, were a risk, but one worth taking for the security they could offer.

Now, at the St Jacques Almonry at Niort, Sutton at last found himself with people as nervous as himself, some of whom had already travelled many miles and had a convincing collection of documents and pilgrim badges, and credible stories of the shrines they had visited. At Niort, the road from Nantes converged with that from the north-east, bringing travellers from central Normandy, pilgrims from Flanders and Brabant, farther Germany and Sweden, who had crossed the Loire at Saumur. Some had come through Brandenburg, and seen the miraculous Hosts of Wilsnack, three altar breads which alone had survived the burning of the church and were found among the ashes, spotted with blood. Others had begun their journey near Cologne, praying at the golden shrines of the Three Kings, whose relics were taken there from Constantinople by the Emperor Frederick Barbarossa. Thence their road led to Aachen, another city of pilgrims, who went there to see the smock the Virgin had worn at Christ's birth, the swaddling clothes, the loin cloth that Christ wore on the Cross, and the cloth used to carry away John the Baptist's severed head. Those pilgrims who wished to travel on from Aachen, to the numerous shrines of France, could go via Paris, now recovering from the years of chaos and a prolonged and bloody siege and with a well-established Confraternity for the care of pilgrims, and take the Orléans or Chartres roads. Or they could keep west to Le Mans where an equally large, prosperous and highly organized Confraternity of St Jacques waited to care for them, to restore them and set them on their way again fortified and armed with the latest news of the road. These confraternities, becoming established all over France, were vital to the exchange of information so necessary for pilgrims: what credence to give to local rumours, stories relayed by travellers coming in the opposite direction, reassurance or warnings about the state of the roads and bridges, the activity of particular criminal bands. Like hubs of overlapping wheels, they kept relevant and reliable information flowing, and by doing so saved uncounted lives.

The pilgrims assembling at Niort were always a mixed bunch. Some were scarcely better than beggars, making the round of the shrines to keep body and soul together. Some were openly sceptical of what they had seen and the extravagant claims of the relics' guardians. Others, shocked at such lack of respect, were soberly pious, making their pilgrimage for a devout intention, a private vow, or as a penitential exercise. Some were travelling vicariously, being paid to carry out the pilgrimage on behalf of someone else, in fulfilment of a clause in a will. And very occasionally, someone still made a pilgrimage in the hope of a cure, but most of these, hopeless cases for the most part who had given up on conventional medicine, ended their pilgrimage in a hospital ward.

Many nationalities were represented, too. The Germans were curious about each new experience, the crops, the wines, the regional differences in dress and dialect;[3] the Poitevins were understandably nervous of foreigners, especially Normans and Burgundians, and exaggerated their patois so they remained a cohesive group, cold-shouldering outsiders. The Flemings and Normans, by contrast, spoke languages Sutton could understand. The priests and monks were mostly on a limited leave of absence, and travelled mounted in the hope of making better speed.[4] Among the laity, some rode in groups, but others were like Sutton, walking alone.

Two days down the road from Niort was a stop that they would all make. St John the Baptist was a key figure in the Christian pageant of saints. His feast day at midsummer was a time for general rejoicings and bonfires, and his role as the Forerunner of Christ assured him a place in popular devotion. Sutton had already seen the Baptist's pointing finger at Mottisfont, and here at St Jean d'Angély was his skull, cut from his body by order of King Herod. Presented to the Benedictine abbey by Pepin, who had received it as a gift from Alexandria, the skull had been treasured here for generations, making the abbey one of the largest and wealthiest in France. At the height of its prestige, this relic and its cult supported 'a hundred monks ... and wrought countless miracles. While the head was being transported by sea and by land it gave many proofs of its miraculous power: on the sea it warded off numerous perils, and on the land it brought dead men back to life. Accordingly it is believed to be indeed the head of the venerable Forerunner.'[5]

The fifteenth century was not such a credulous age as the twelfth, or perhaps too many implausible 'relics' had been hawked about, so belief was wearing thin. There were certainly some who harboured reservations as to the authenticity of this particular relic. It was quite well known that visitors to Constantinople were shown the back portion of St John's skull, said to have been kept there when the front part was sent to Rome. The lower jaw was exhibited in Genoa, and other pilgrims had been shown the entire skull in Picardy. But St Jean d'Angély had a very long tradition of claiming the Baptist's head, backed up by a royal donor and many miracles in the abbey. Much the safest course in such cases was to treat all relics with the reverence the real one would merit. As Sir John Mandeville wrote: 'I wot never, but God knoweth. But in what wise that men worship it the blessed St John holdeth him apaid.'[6]

There were limits to the wisdom of this approach, of course. No merit could be gained from revering the tiny skulls displayed as 'the head of St John in infancy'. Far too many charlatans, often in holy orders, were battening on the poor and taking advantage of their ignorance and fear by displaying 'relics' that were manifestly fraudulent. Geoffrey Chaucer had been right to hold them up to ridicule in his description of the Pardoner:

> *With him ther rood a gentil pardoner*
> *Of Rouncival …*
> *But of his craft, fro Berwik into Ware,*
> *Ne was ther swich another pardoner.*
> *For in his male he hadde a pilwe-beer [pillow-case],*
> *Which that, he seyde, was our lady veyl:*
> *He seyde, he hadde a gobet of the seyl*
> *That seynt Peter hadde, whan that he wente*
> *Up-on the see, til Iesu Crist him hente.*
> *He hadde a croys of latoun, ful of stones,*
> *And in a glas he hadde pigges bones.*
> *But with thise relikes, whan that he fond*
> *A poure person [parson] dwelling up-on lond,*
> *Up-on a day he gat him more moneye*
> *Than that the person gat in monthes tweye.*
> *And thus, with feyned flaterye and Iapes,*
> *He made the person and the peple his apes.*[7]

As time went on, more people were beginning to wonder about even the well-established relics. Fewer pilgrims were visiting shrines like St Jean d'Angély, miracles seldom occurred there and the abbey establishment had shrunk to a fraction of its former size. Most telling of all, perhaps, the great Forerunner had manifestly failed to protect the town from the dangers that had assailed it recently.

16

Troubled Times

The monastery of St John at Angély . . . is suffering considerable ruin and the harvests of this monastery stand very greatly diminished because of the said wars.[1]

St Jean d'Angély had troubles of its own. After weeks crossing old war zones and seeing towns still freshly scarred, here Sutton found a city unhealed from past conflicts and grimly bracing itself for more. When he set off from home at Easter, he had no concept of the effect of the decades of fighting in France, nor how much it would affect his own pilgrimage. Now he was confronted by new wars and rumours of war, coming up from the south to meet him.

St Jean d'Angély Abbey, badly mauled and even temporarily abandoned, had scarcely recovered in the 50-year interlude since the English were driven out of the region.[2] Then the tide of war had begun to turn again, and in 1412 an Anglo-Gascon army crossed the River Charente and besieged Taillebourg, only four leagues away. Suddenly, St Jean had found itself uncomfortably close to the front line once more. The townsmen strengthened the walls as best they could, and demolished all the extramural buildings, including several of their seven pilgrim hostels, to eliminate cover for hostile troops. A permanent watch, 80 strong, was ordered, and the French Crown had sent down two great guns from the north to assist in the defence. Then, when it seemed certain that the town would be caught up in the fighting, the Duke of Bourbon abruptly switched sides, and swept down upon the unsuspecting Anglo-Gascons, who discovered too late that he was no longer their ally. He liberated Taillebourg, destroyed its castle lest it fall into enemy hands, and pushed the demoralized Gascons far back south towards Bordeaux.

St Jean d'Angély was unable to take advantage of this respite to rebuild or reinforce. The abbey suffered 'because of lack of workers that the resources have been so much reduced because of the wars that the fabric of the buildings can only be held up through a decrease in the number of staff . . . the Cellarer complains that he is obliged to keep secure the refectory, the cloister, the granaries and other houses and to repair the walls of the monastery, but there are no resources'.[3] Meanwhile 'the priory of St James of Mercies outside the walls of the town of St John at Angély . . . is collapsed in its structures and buildings because of the wars and . . . has been flattened to the ground so completely',[4] and 'The hospice for the infirm poor and pilgrims in the House of St John at Angély . . . so diminished in incomes because of the war etc. that it cannot provide for the poor.'[5] Everywhere, it seemed, was disaster; labourers fled, fields uncultivated, rents unpaid, ancient church buildings falling into ruin or deliberately destroyed in the interests of war.

In August 1420 Sir John Tiptoft arrived at Bordeaux with a convoy of ships commandeered at Bristol, bringing reinforcements, weapons, food and above all a new spirit to the Anglo-Gascons and their wavering allies. In November 1420 the Armagnacs had been at Pons, threatening the approaches to Bordeaux, but the newly courageous Gascons pushed north again. By August 1421 St Jean d'Angély was so vulnerable to their approach that the city refused to send a contingent north to swear obedience to the dauphin, though whether military or diplomatic calculations predominated it was hard to be sure.

In the town, a frenzy of work began on the defences, 'pour le doubte des Anglois'. The two heavy guns were mounted on specially constructed platforms, one above the southern Taillebourg Gate, the

other by the Matha Gate to the east, and they were supplied with
rounds of home-made stone shot. The road in under the west gate
was improved and paved, and its drawbridge repaired. In April 1423
the mayor, Hélie de Saumur, called a council meeting which attracted
52 members, who readily agreed to impose a full watch on the walls
and to pay for further work on the west gate. On Friday 14 May, a
further council assembly reiterated the need for a full-scale alert, and
urged yet more effort to repair the town bridges, gates and walls.[6]

In such a climate of raw fear, the arrival of a party of pilgrims was
a mixed blessing. Where they would normally have represented one
tiny element in a complex, profitable and well-established tradition
at the heart of St Jean's prosperity, now they were a drain on
resources, a distraction from urgent concerns and a potential threat.
Yet they were accommodated, to the best of the town's ability. The
salt trade and the wine trade were so disrupted that only pilgrims
offered additional revenues, and their care remained a primary
obligation. So in a curiously ambivalent atmosphere, the party was
shepherded in through the Niort Gate, to whichever almonry could
best provide them with bread and wine, and out again under the Sin
Tower through the Matha Gate to the Almonry of St Michael, where
some sort of lodging could still be offered, and where the big gun on
its hastily built chevelet glared out at them over the moat.

Next day, as soon as the Matha Gate was opened by its cautious
guard, they were free to go in to the abbey in the centre of the town.
Their worship done and their offerings at the shrine of St John's
head gratefully accepted, they were ushered promptly out down the
central street to the Taillebourg Gate, over the four branches of the
River Boutonne and past the sad remnants of the St Jacques Priory
and the Maladrerie St Lazare, both incapable of offering much to
travellers, except the most despairing.

Past splendid and miraculously still functioning Fenioux Priory,
and on down a pleasant valley route to the river crossing at
Taillebourg, the journey threw another kind of trouble at a mind
distressed by the conflicting messages at St Jean. For weeks, Sutton's
determination to be true to his pilgrimage had been held against a
backdrop of loneliness. Memories of happy bands of pilgrims
coming through Worcester homeward bound from distant shrines,

united groups, caring groups, had sustained him and urged him to seek company. Now he found himself part of a group, and the dream had curdled like milk on a summer's day. If he walked at the front, those at the rear dawdled intolerably. At the rear, the vanguard sped away unthinkingly while he was held up by the slow ones at every obstacle on the road, and they, ignoring promises made, began walking again as soon as the stragglers caught up. To walk in the middle, or where the road was wide enough for the party to bunch together as one, exposed him to endless attempts at gossip which, whether profane, pious or merely banal, cut across his own thoughts and quickly drove him to distraction. For the more introspective pilgrims, this new dimension became a wrestling match with profound ill will at added complications on a journey already overstocked with trouble.

Taillebourg was clutching at its tatters of self-respect, its once-proud castle now reduced to ruins, with only half of its keep still standing. Down the steep main street to the River Charente, and over the precarious remains of the bridge, the party made its way along a causeway 'over a long marsh across many small stone bridges', to the hamlet of St James.[7] There, at least, some semblance of normality returned, in the pilgrim hospice close by the road, where uncertain marsh became firm ground again.

If the situation at St Jean was confusing and distressing, the sights that greeted them at Saintes were harder by far to grasp, despite the warnings of north-bound travellers they met on the way. Once a proud city and regional capital, poor sad Saintes was brought low by accident and war. The extramural Priory of St Vivien had lost three-quarters of its revenues, the city's staple exports of wine, corn and luxury decorated Saintogne Ware jugs were decimated by the depopulation of the countryside, and most of the mills along the once-busy waterfront were standing idle. Part of the Cathedral of St Pierre had collapsed abruptly in May 1420 'and one man died and a hundred thousand would if they had been there ... the church was built on top of a certain lake where the bodies of very many holy martyrs had earlier been cast, and had fallen down due to a defect in its foundations'.[8] Above the city, up streets so steep they were stepped, the Cluniac church of St Eutrope, once the largest church in the Saintogne, was reduced from 20 rich monks to 10 impoverished ones, and its hospice, which had always been a reliable place for pilgrims to stay, was unable to help them. The canons had appealed to the pope for help in 1418, but in 1420 part of the church fell down, and five years later it was 'utterly let go to ruin', with resources 'not sufficient to sustain divine worship'.[9] Whether they had come to venerate the relics of St Eutrope, holy martyr and founder of the Christian church in Saintes, or whether they were en route for Compostela and other distant shrines, the city was not the spiritual and emotional high-point the pilgrims had anticipated, but a disappointing trawl through impoverished and ruinous almonries and inns, past closed and derelict churches, to buy a pilgrim badge and scrape together what provisions they could find before pressing on.

At Pons for the eve of Holy Trinity, they found a hospice still in reasonable repair, and able to offer more help. With its claustral buildings to one side, and pilgrim accommodation on the other, linked by a sheltering arch, it was a clear reminder that whatever the loyalties of the Seigneur, the care of pilgrims had a life and a value of its own, wherever means permitted.

Once south of Pons, there seemed a real possibility of reaching the security of lands held for England, despite the disturbing way that every low wave of the gently undulating landscape seemed to reveal an ever more wooded vista, a foretaste of the great forests of the Baconais and the Landes which stretched patchily from here to the foothills of the mountains. No sooner was one danger beginning to fade away than another reared its head. There was a vast tract of land ahead, partially cleared for vines and cereals, but still enough of a forest for wild animals to abound: bears, wolves and boars, and the occasional lynx that preyed fearlessly on sheep and goats if the herdsmen relaxed their watch. In years gone by, the clearings in these northern fringes of the forest had been fertile and productive, yielding abundant surpluses for the numerous Hospitaller priories, but the area had been torn between opposing factions for far too long, and many farms and villages were now abandoned. As a final turn of the screw, the suffering people had twice been laid low by major resurgences of pestilence in the last ten years. The conventional invocation of the Holy Trinity against plagues gave a particular cohesion to the pilgrimage on this Trinity Sunday.

Hurrying on along the broad road south, it was some comfort to find a succession of abbeys and priories, impoverished but still functioning: Belluire St Jacques with its hospice; La Tenaille Abbey which displayed a nail from the crucifixion and the pincers used to draw it out; and St Martin's Priory at Petit Niort, guarded by the Mirambeau castle. A little farther on again, there was Pleine Selve Abbey down in a fold of a valley below the road, surrounded by the countless oak and pine trees (*plena sylva*, 'the abundance of trees'), patiently working its heathland soils made productive by years of labour. It was an oasis of vineyards and corn in the wilderness, and a friendly roof for the night.[10]

PART VI

Gascony

17

Ferry over the Gironde

Vasconia, that is Gasguyne, ... hath in the est side the hilles Pyrenei, in the west the west ocean ... In that lond beeth meny woodes, hilles, and vynes; and the ryver Garonna departeth by twene that lond and the province of Tholous, and entreth into the see of occean fast by Burdeux; that is the chief citee of that lond.[1]

From Pleine Selve to the Gironde was just one day's journey, with enemies at bay, the warm sun shining and clear roads with hospices and churches spread out comfortingly along the way. The Hospitallers at St-Martin-la-Caussade[2] were a most useful final fall-back a half-league short of the end, but for most pilgrims the incentive to be at the shore by dusk was enough to spur them on to one final effort for the day. For the last hour or so, the waters of the great estuary could be glimpsed over to the right, but not until the final descent towards Blaye did the real scale of it strike home, a sight that even familiarity could not wholly rob of its power, and one that caused first-time travellers to pause in awestruck wonder. The islands far out in mid-stream dwarfed the busy shipping, but the farther shore was more remote by far, misty with distance. To the right, the great curving arm of water, golden in the setting sun, swept on until it vanished from sight, ever wider with still no sign of the open sea.

Blaye was a city of strange echoes, odd confusions of ancient tales, part pilgrim home, part frontier fortress. The Hôpital de la Lande, so conveniently situated by the road in from the north, a place where pilgrims were welcomed and fed so well on fresh fish from the estuary and rich Blaye wine, had been founded long ago by Jaufré Rudel, Lord of Blaye. Earlier still, another Jaufré Rudel had lived in the castle, composing poetry and songs and entertaining pilgrims and crusaders returning from the Holy Land. From them, he had learned of the beautiful Countess of Tripoli, a paragon of virtues for whom he wrote and sang until he was torn with an aching desire to see her. Eventually, so the story went, Rudel took the Cross, but fell mortally ill on the boat, and was taken off and abandoned at an inn in Tripoli. There the Countess came to him in compassion for a dying Christian, and nursed him until he died in her arms. He was buried there by the Knights Templar, and the Countess took the veil in his memory. This ancient tale of distant longing struck a sympathetic chord in the hearts of the votaries of St James.

Pilgrims came to Blaye for two reasons. It controlled the narrows across the estuary, offering a relatively safe crossing point, and it had two abbeys, housing important relics. The royal castle and strongly fortified town, up on a crag above the harbour, watched over a place where the waters narrowed to half a league; by guarding this strategic point it served as the key to Bordeaux, out of sight far up-river. Here at last Sutton was again protected by an English garrison, in a town whose obedience was directly to Henry VI as Duke of Guyenne. The rebel armies had pulled back far to the north, Anglo-Gascon morale was high and the town seemed secure.

But many scars remained, some lingering unhealed. Neither of the abbeys had recovered from a grievous sacking three generations earlier; the Benedictines of St Sauveur's were completely demoralized and impoverished, their buildings almost deserted, and the few remaining brothers destitute and dismayed. The Augustinians at St Romain's, hard by the east gate, still had some income from their pilgrim trade, and had at first fared a little better. But in the uncertain years just after the Lancastrian coup, when many in Gascony still favoured Richard II and may have expected his restoration, their abbot had, foolishly as it turned out, decided to open the city gates to a French faction. Blaye was swiftly retaken, and in reprisal the furious pro-English soldiery wrecked the St Romain Abbey. Only the holiest relics were spared. The Augustinians had worked hard to promote their treasures as an important facet of the Compostelan pilgrimage experience; now they were all that was left to them. So Sutton and his companions were eagerly taken through the vandalized abbey, and shown the tombs of 'St Apollonia and St Romanus, a bishop, also the tomb of Roland ... also St Oliver ... St Belanda'.[3] Also on display to interested pilgrims was a great horn, Roland's Olifant with which he had tried, too late, to summon the Christian army of Charlemagne against the Moslems of Spain. Pilgrimage, self-sacrifice and Crusade: a heady mixture to give meaning to Blaye and to feed its dreams.

Back on the prosaic streets, Sutton confronted the estuary over which Blaye stood sentinel. How was it to be crossed? There were three options, each with its own dangers. The long way, but the easiest in years of peace, was to walk up the coast past Bourg to Cubzac, and there cross a broad river by ferry. A second day's walk past more abbeys and castles brought one at length to an even wider river, the Garonne, and a second ferry to Bordeaux on the farther shore. But the Armagnacs were still threatening part of this route, and the abbeys had suffered greatly, so their resources were sadly diminished. Although the situation was improving, this option was not recommended. An alternative, taken by the wealthy, was to embark at Blaye and travel by boat to Bordeaux, carried up on a single tide. With an experienced pilot, the many sandbanks and shoals could be safely avoided, but it was not cheap, and people were nervous of pirate raids. Better to make a short crossing from Blaye, to the Médoc shore opposite, which had never wavered in its allegiance, never suffered occupation, and walk on to Bordeaux on that side.

There were no large vessels in the estuary, and its breadth further dwarfed those there were, but there were ferrymen in plenty. Since time immemorial this had been a crossing point, and every sandbank and eddy and trick of the tides was known to the mariners like the scars and knots on their own brown hands. For this was a river estuary unlike any the pilgrims had seen before. Wider by far than the Severn, wider than the great rivers the Germans and Swedes had crossed, wider even than the Loire at Nantes. And its water was not blue or green or even grey, like the sea, but an unfathomable muddy brown. Kites hovered and swooped over the city and shoreline as they went cautiously on board, and the swirling turbid water merged imperceptibly on either side into mudbanks and islands, shaped by the tides that ebbed and flowed all day. Blaye was already a hazy blur in the distance behind them before any detail could be made out on the coastline ahead, but then it gradually drew nearer, accompanied by many anxious prayers. The tide had turned before the boat nosed into the bank, and a score of relieved pilgrims disembarked on a rough jetty over the grey slimy mudbanks of the Médoc foreshore.

Almost at once, the feeling of being in a new country was palpable, as if the world had changed shape. Here there was no visible war damage. Vines were in full growth, well tended and luxuriant; whatever pestilences had come, the wine trade was profitable enough to pay for labourers to tend the crop. The castles that watched the shore were status symbols as much as for defence, and at Arcins, the Hospitallers had a well-equipped commandery, mother-house to St-Martin-la-Caussade by Blaye, which maintained the ford and had food and wine enough and to spare.

From Arcins, there was just one more day's journey to Bordeaux, city of safety, of holy relics, of English law and order, and the end of so many fears. The road ran close to the shoreline for the most part, on this day that was St Elmo's day and the eve of Corpus Christi. A series of sturdy castles enhanced the sense of security and well-being; they guarded the road more determinedly here, closer to the estuary water, more military in intention. The events of the last few years had shown that pirate raids thrusting for the heart of Bordeaux were no idle threat: some had penetrated well above Blaye, and although no lasting damage had been done, some uncomfortable weaknesses had been exposed. In 1405, Castilian galleys had sailed right up to Bordeaux, until

More than a hundred boats and cutters manned by men-at-arms came out from among the ships, and shot so many arrows and bolts at the galleys that those therein had enough to do to fight and defend themselves. There were four castles on the city side and very near it, and the captain ordered men to go to burn them. Then many men on foot and mounted came out in arms from the city to defend these castles; but they could not get there soon enough to prevent them from being all burnt. The galleys reached the other side of the shore and the captain ordered all the houses and all the corn (of which there was much in this part) to be fired, and whosoever they found there to be killed and plundered, so that in a few hours more than a hundred and fifty houses were in flames. The captain would have liked to remain some days in the Gironde to wreak more harm ... but he had news that the English fleet was then expected ... One galley would have gone aground if God had not willed to save her ...[4]

Since these alarming events, the tide of war had swung in Bordeaux's favour. The castles, especially mighty Blanquefort which stood on the very edge of the coastal marshes, protecting the city from the north, were still vigilant and watchful, but in the fields confidence had returned. Wheat crops were being replaced with new vineyards as the old assurance and profitability came back, and the prime sites at Margaux and Macau were flourishing once more. South of Blanquefort, too, with the walls of Bordeaux already in sight, there were vines, planted right up to the gates and encircling the city in an arc of plenty.

18

Blessed Bordeaux

To Burdewez, to that faire citee,
And there was I daies thre.[1]

Bordeaux, splendid, vast and prosperous, was itself all on tiptoe with anticipation for the great festival of Corpus Christi. The city was unimaginably big; the walls were a league in circumference, so it would take a full hour just to walk around the perimeter. Inside, the people bustled and shouted and hurried to be ready for the festival to begin. The population, ten times that of Worcester, was as varied as it was vibrant, a mixture of ship owners, wine and cloth merchants, grain dealers, dock workers, cask makers, craftsmen and clergy of all sorts and conditions. Most were Anglo-Gascons, but there were any number of other accents to be heard: the broad familiar English of the Bristol merchants and their factors, the sharper London speech, sailors and traders from half the outlandish ports of the world, and an assortment of erstwhile pilgrims and others who had chosen to settle here rather than face whatever awaited them at home.

It was all too easy to lose the way at first, but there were plenty of kindly people on the streets who could direct a multilingual group of pilgrims to the Hospital of St James. Down the rue des Jacobins, through the inner gate into the heart of the old city, past churches, more gates and redundant inner walls, through the main city market place, and out under a fine clock tower along rue St James to the newest part of the city out to the south. Founded and richly endowed by the Dukes of Aquitaine,[2] the hospital was run by a community of Augustinian brothers expressly for 'pilgrims going and returning on the journey to St James in Galicia so they can be accommodated and fed'.[3] The able-bodied were given shelter, the sick were nursed, and the dying were cared for and then buried in the adjacent cemetery, linked for ever with their pilgrimage. There were many other hospitals in Bordeaux: the Antonines, the Brothers of Mercy, two Hospitaller houses, La Peste, several lazars and the newly endowed city hospital of St André with 26 beds set aside for the medical care of the sick; all these and more, besides the guest houses of the numerous priories and convents. But only St James's was reserved exclusively for Compostelan pilgrims, and there they first made their way.

The next day, Thursday, was Corpus Christi, a day of exuberant communal rejoicing and civic pride. A day also for regrouping and drawing new inspiration from the liturgy and sacrament. Sutton had seen pieces of the True Cross on this pilgrimage; he had seen the Nail at La Tenaille; he was travelling with people who had seen the loin cloth of the Crucifixion, at Aachen. He had also been forced to ponder long and hard on the experience of pain, hunger, thirst, rejection and misunderstanding. Now at the Corpus Christi Mass, the link was made explicit:

Ave verum Corpus natum
De Maria Virgine
Vere passum, immolatum
In cruce pro homine.

Cujus latus perforatum
Fluxit aqua et sanguine,
Esto nobis praegustatum
Mortis in examine.[4]

And new meaning suffused the beautiful familiar hymns of the festival, for Sutton and for the hundreds of pilgrims like him, gathered together that morning in the cathedral and in churches and chapels across the city:

Ecce, panis Angelorum,
Factus cibus viatorum ...[5]

After Mass, the Sacrament was carried through the city, preceded by processional crosses and accompanied by clergy, choirs and city dignitaries, the mayor and members of the Jurade council in their magnificent scarlet and blood-red livery, contrasting with the crisp white vestments of the clerics. At each of the numerous temporary altars erected along the route, the Sacrament was placed reverently down while a passage of the Gospels was sung, followed by prayers for the city, its people and its prosperity. All along the way, the occupants of the houses lining the route came out to watch and worship, and knelt in the street as the Holy Body came past and blessed their neighbourhood. And at every stage, the people sang the Corpus Christi hymn of St Thomas, until it seemed to echo back from every corner:

Panis angelicus, fit panis hominum;
Dat panis caelicus figuris terminum;

O res mirabilis! Manducat Dominum
Pauper, servus, et humilis![6]

Then, when the procession had wound its way far out of sight and
nearly beyond hearing, there was time for Sutton to visit the great
relics of the city before the plays and feasting began. Out past the
huge 'Pillars of Tutelle'[7] and through the Jewish Gate, he followed a
stream of fellow pilgrims all making their way to and from one
destination, where 'outside the town westwards, at St Surin, in the
church, lies St Severinus: half of him is in a beautiful shrine. They
say the other half is at Cologne.'[8] The church had been left outside
the enlarged city walls, in a warren of streets that had once been the
Jewish suburb. Perhaps the decision to leave it thus had been taken
through fear of diseases the pilgrims might carry, or uncertainty
because the Jews had then only recently been expelled from the
English domains, or perhaps lest the pilgrimage become a cover for
enemy action. Whatever the reason, St Seurin's had not suffered in
consequence; indeed, it seemed to revel in its special extramural
status. A whole panoply of treasures was there, an armoury for all
the varied battles of life. The dean and 24 canons of the church
maintained a vigorous parish ministry, 'seeing to the ringing of the
bells . . . oil and wax for the appointed wax lights, lamps and torches
that are burning day and night and keeping two clerks from divine
service to sound the bells, light the candles and keep watch and also
to assist diligently in carrying the Body of Christ for the parish and
other accustomed services . . .'[9]

Among the many holy bodies said to be there were St Veronica,
the bishop-martyrs Severinus and Amandus and, confusingly for
pilgrims who had just come from Blaye, Roland and several of his
Twelve Companions. The church also displayed a broken ivory horn,
said to be the Oliphant, cracked asunder when Roland blew his last
mighty blast upon it as his enemies closed in. But if the collegiate
church of St Seurin was in dispute with the Augustinians of Blaye
over which was the true Oliphant, there was no rival claim to the
body of St Fort, one of the 72 disciples sent out by Christ, whose
undisputed burial place was here at Bordeaux.[10] Each year in May,
mothers brought their sickly children and placed them on his tomb

so that they might grow up fit and strong, and those with eye diseases were annointed with St Fort's water, with miraculous effects. St Seurin's also owned the Rod of St Martial, given to him by St Peter himself, a rod which worked 'various and very evident miracles ... a great multitude of the people has been accustomed to gather year by year from ancient times to make their devotions on particular days, ... and especially on the day after the Nativity and the Resurrection of Our Lord and Pentecost'.[11] This Rod was traditionally used in the ceremonial arming of English Gascon war-leaders before battle, and the church was proud of its unswerving loyalty to the Duke-King. Last but far from least, in a side chapel stood the statue of Our Lady of the Good Tidings, a fine English alabaster that was the focus of a cult in its own right, a poignant and paradoxical image of Mother and Child, with the Spirit-bird tearing at her heart.

Meanwhile, back in the city, the festivities of Corpus Christi changed key, with feasting and drinking for all: meat pies, fresh trout from the river, asparagus (a local delicacy), and the excellent Bordeaux wine at a fraction of the price it could be obtained in England. And later, there was an outdoor mystery play, retelling the story of man's fall and most glorious redemption.[12]

On the following morning, Bordeaux was still celebrating. But for pilgrims it was time to be moving on. The Confraternity of St James advised getting extra documents, obtainable from the royal castle of the Ombrière. So, after an offering for a light at the new statue of St James at their chapel in St Michael's church,[13] Sutton went up to the northern limits of the city, where after a long wait the duty officer at the castle checked his bona fides with care, throwing in pertinent questions about the route he had taken across Poitou and the things he had noticed on the way. Then he was issued with a safe-conduct, valid for the summer, for going and returning to St James. Those pilgrims who had arrived by boat, direct to Bordeaux or walking through the Médoc from Soulac on the coast, were issued with one safe-conduct for the whole party, and were expected to travel on to Compostela in company. Fortunately for Sutton, he was able to choose his own companions for the road, and could opt for a smaller group, which would surely be quicker and might make accommodation easier to find.

With their new safe-conducts stowed carefully in their scrips, Sutton and a few companions left the castle and traversed the waterfront area, by the wide river busy with little ships and rowing boats. At its upstream end, beyond St Michael's, they turned away from the river, past the Benedictines of Sainte Croix, past the Poor Clares, past the Augustinians, and out through the Porte d'Aquitaine into the southern suburbs. They were advised to be clear of the city well before dark, to spend the night at one of the many extramural hospices and thereby cut an hour or two from their first day's journey over the Great Heath of the Landes that lay ahead.

Just outside the gate, as the road swung to the right, they passed the house of St Julian, set among the remnants of a leper colony. It was an unpleasant reminder of the large part leprosy had once played in people's lives, and a sign that here in Gascony it was still all too common. The guest house 'for pilgrims going to and returning from St James and for others of Christ's poor who gathered there . . . after the city gates have been shut at night' was all the more necessary in order to keep benighted travellers from contact with the foul disease.[14]

Keeping well clear of the lepers, the pilgrims crossed a rich area of vineyards that surrounded the village of St Geniès, and noted with pleasure the large stone cross that told them that they were on the 'royal and public road through which Christians set out on pilgrimage to the blessed James at Compostela'.[15] More vines, more tiny plots of land around the village of Talence, and then they passed the once-wealthy guest house of St Mary at Bardenac.[16] At Gradignan they found a village with a more rural and independent air; new-mown hay lay in the fields, and a patchwork of vegetable plots rubbed shoulders with the vineyards. There was a rustic statue of St James in the church to encourage them on, and it was only another half-hour before they reached the grand Hospitaller Priory of Cayac, with church on one side and hospice on the other, linked by a great arch over the road. A rich and confident house, closely identified with the Compostelan route, it was almost untouched by the wars. With a flourishing Confraternity of St James, it had burial rights, a large pilgrim cemetery by the church, and an ancilliary lazar house. In the morning, the pilgrims could begin to tackle the Great Heath, but for now they were safely lodged, two hours south of Bordeaux.

19

The Road through the Landes

I was come into a plentiful country; for Aquitainy hath no felow for good wyne & bred.[1]

To the many pilgrims who came by boat to Bordeaux and started their overland trek from there, the Landes may have seemed like the hostile heath of the old stories: a four-day wilderness with no cities nor even any significant towns; a rigorous four-day introduction to the realities of travel on foot, impelled to move on daily by the pressure of other pilgrims following them down the road. But to Sutton it was merely an interlude, a transition between Bordeaux with its soaring spiritual high point of Corpus Christi, and the mountains that he knew lay ahead. Unscathed by war, spared many of the pestilences that had denuded the cities and the more populous regions, the Landes were more secure than any region of the continent he had yet seen. Clearings in the oak and pine forests provided for a surprisingly large rural population; the grey sandy soil grew vines, rye, millet, wheat and vegetables, the oakwoods fattened fine pigs, and the pastures, scented now with new-mown hay, supported flocks of sheep, duck and geese.[2] Even the former hardships of travel in the region had worked in its favour, with so many bequests for hospices that almost every village now had a pilgrim refuge of some sort, and the main axes of movement were well supplied with priories, hospitals and chapels of many different Orders.[3]

The priory hospital of Le Barp, with its enclosure symbolically marked by four huge crosses which had themselves become a traditional goal of pilgrims, was a long day's walk for those unaccustomed to the road.[4] Sutton and his smaller party, hardened and more determined, could press on another hour and a half to the hospital of St Esprit outside Belin-Béliet. The small royal castle there guarded the road as it bent and descended to cross the River Leyre, and a mound was pointed out to pilgrims (rather optimistically) as the burial place of Olivier and the Companions. A more likely and equally stirring story was that Queen Eleanor, mother of the Lionheart, had been born in the castle.

Although there were many places for pilgrims to stay in the Landes, care was still needed towards nightfall. The question of where and when to stop was compounded by misunderstandings over distances: 'miles' and 'leagues' were used by many nations, but it soon became apparent that ideas of how long they were differed radically. To Sutton a league was an hour's walk in the barely undulating Landes, where there were few streams to slow him down. But travelling in an international party, and asking for information from local Gascons, the situation became complex to the point of absurdity. 'In German lands the miles with which we are familiar are generally an hour's riding for one mile. In Lombardy, in Italy, five miles equals a German mile, and in other foreign countries such as Savoy, Biscay, Gascony, Spain and France, they are called leagues, but they are reckoned differently: sometimes two leagues makes a [German] mile, sometimes three, and at times four make a mile ...'[5]

So, following a road that was clear enough, but never knowing how long it would prove to be, Sutton and his party pressed on, past hamlets, churches and castles: Mons, Le Muret, Liposthey, in a landscape turning hot and dry for summer. Birdsong bounced back off the sky, accompanied by the sharp cracking of the pine cones. At Labouheyre, by the river, a castle and fortified town ensured that merchants halted to pay their tolls, while pilgrims passed freely on under their safe-conducts. The Carmelites had a big convent and hospital here, at the very heart of the Landes, midway between Bordeaux and Dax, in a town planted, as it were, out in the forests, owing its whole existence to the pilgrimage and the castle on the road.

Near Escource, and again the following night at Poymartet after a long and weary day's march, Sutton was sheltered by the Antonines. St Antoine de la Traverse by Escource was only a small house, but stood in an area long famous for its healing springs, dedicated variously to St Antony, St Martin, St Lô and St Rufine. Down at Poymartet, the brick-built St Jacques Priory was larger, with beds for 36 men and 36 women in the hospital, a separate space for children, a ward reserved for the victims of St Antony's fire in bad years, and a cemetery and chapel. The priory farm easily fed and clothed the staff of five and their lay helpers, as well as their many guests, and Sutton could sleep that night under linen sheets and a woollen blanket, on a luxurious mattress stuffed with goose and duck feathers from the priory flocks. The road was so busy, and demands on their time so great, that the Antonines had built the hospital close to the road, but set their own buildings back apart, to help preserve their necessary spiritual calm. Thus they were able to minister to the thousands who passed their doors each year, without becoming lost in the noise and business of the work. Poymartet, the 'high hammer' of St Antony, was a model of the best sort of care for pilgrims, whatever their needs.[6]

The last few leagues to Dax were much more varied, with pleasant streams gurgling through meadows that cut wide swathes across the oak woods, like England at high summer. At St-Paul-les-Dax they crossed a little stone bridge and came down to the Adour, a river of the same temper as the Severn, deep and wide, with a hospice and suburb on the near side and a great fortress on the other, across a long wooden bridge. Here again the cavalcades of merchants had to pay tolls, while bona fide pilgrims passed freely on over the bridge into the city, to gaze at the steam rising from the piping-hot fountain and to give thanks at the cathedral for a safe crossing of the Landes.

Dax was fervently loyal to the English Crown, a good place to spend a day before tackling the mountains, whose foothills began to rise up in ever-increasing waves almost from the gates of the city. And if the Judgement Portal of the cathedral, just finished and set in a building where new construction work was going on apace, was a sobering reminder that the outcome of this pilgrimage was not assured, the prominent presence of St Andrew and St James on either side of that same doorway was a comforting reassurance to Sutton that he was not travelling unaided.

One day at Dax to draw breath, spend a couple of nights at one of its hospices, get boots repaired and feet bathed in the healing pools fed by the bubbling springs, and they were on their way again, up past St Pandelon and Pouillon, through the hilly, wooded countryside that led to Sorde l'Abbaye and on towards the Kingdom of Navarre.

PART VII

Navarre

20
Echoes of Roland

Between St Jean Pied de Port and Pamplona lie the ravines and canyons of Navarre, which are most dangerous to pass through, for there are a hundred places among them where a whole army could be held up by thirty men.[1]

Sorde was a magnificent Benedictine abbey, fortified, rich and kind to pilgrims. It stood on the near bank of the Gave d'Oloron, a chilling mountain river of terrible reputation, now tamed by the labours of the brothers of Sorde. The sick were taken into the abbey hospital, under the care of the prior almoner, but fit pilgrims were directed down to the little extramural hospital at Espitaou, a few minutes away. It only had five beds, but its rock-cut vaults were full of cider and wine, and there were two full-time staff, a prior hospitaller and a widow who was employed specifically to look after the linen. Equally encouraging, right next to the hospital, just beyond its archway, was a bridge across the rushing river, leading to the old ferry house on the farther shore.[2]

As in the Landes, so too in these foothills with their deep-cut riverbeds: the difficulties of the journey, both real and imagined, had spawned so many pious donations that every hamlet now seemed to offer help to pilgrims, or an inn where merchants and travellers could stay. But here, unlike in the Landes, there were so many little valleys converging and bifurcating, so many alternative routes presenting themselves, that it was often unclear which path to take. Individual settlements were often small, and the sheer volume of pilgrims was beginning to be so great, that big parties were now obliged to make disciplined halts at prescribed intervals. For Sutton and his companions, by contrast, there seemed an almost limitless choice, and the days could be as long or as short as the changing needs of individuals demanded.

From Sorde via Ordios they came to Arancou, which proved to be their last Gascon town. There they had a choice of two hospitals, one Grandmontine and one a commandery of Roncevaux, a name to lift their spirits and draw them on to the mother-house on the summits ahead. This large Augustinian 'New Hospital of Our Lady of Arancou' stood strategically at the entrance to the village, well endowed and generous to its guests. Indeed, it had such ample lands round about that it sent regular consignments of surplus wine and grain to the almoner's stores at the mother-house in the mountains.[3]

The actual moment when they crossed the border into Navarre could hardly have been more mundane, splashing across the chilly Lauhirasse stream, but the scenery very soon became more challenging, as befitted a mountain kingdom. Past the Grandmontine house at Viellenave-sur-Bidouze, sister-house of the little hospital at Arancou, with its bridge, weir, mill and hospital, past the trim new town of Garris and its castle, imperceptibly the landscape changed, becoming less gentle, more dramatic, with occasional views of the real mountains that lay ahead.

St Palais was not much bigger than Garris,[4] but was a great deal more important. Since 1351, it had been the site of a royal Navarrese mint, an innovation that was transforming a country previously dependent on the currencies of her trading partners, and in consequence the new town now boasted a royal palace, bridges over the two rivers that protected it, and a line of defensive ditches.[5] More significant for pilgrims, St Palais was built close to the priory hospital of St Madeleine of Lagarrague, whose daughter-church of St Paul served the town. The priory stood a little apart, on the old 'high road to St James' that led up the hill to the south. Two hundred years of legacies from wealthy patrons had made Lagarrague a place where it was expected that 'los pobres peregrinos en el dicho ospital pueden ser recogidos e ospedados'.[6]

Above St Palais, the road wound on up the shoulder of St
Salvador hill, which in the curious language of the local Basques was
known as Chalbatore, or Gibraltar. On its summit, consecrating the
whole hill and its surrounding valleys, stood a hermitage, where a
lone monk from the nearby house of Uhart-Mixe kept up a round
of prayers to Our Lady of Mercy of Soyharce, for her protection of
the road, the crops and the fields. In particular, she interceded in
heaven against the hailstorms that could so swiftly flatten a summer
field, destroying the labours of a year and stealing the bread from
the tables of pilgrim and native alike.

Down at the edge of the wooded valley again, past the priory of
Harambeltz, they came to the town of Ostabat, the largest in this
part of Navarre. With a series of streets neatly laid out up the
terraces of the valley side, and numerous hospitals, inns and
chapels, this was a bustling crossroads town, recommended by many
as an ideal place to stay. Ostabat could accommodate an almost
infinitely variable number of people in its assorted establishments.
St Catherine, St Antoine, St Engrâce, St Jean Baptiste, St Juste, St
Saveur and Notre-Dame, all the most reliable patrons of pilgrims
were waiting here to welcome and shelter suppliants, and the fertile
fields of the valley floor provided abundant apples, pears, cider, milk
and grain for travellers rich and poor.[7]

By now, the trickle of pilgrims was becoming a steady stream,
despite the multiplicity of tracks. Each side valley fed in from other
roads across the hills, where other unseen priories nursed more
travellers on their way. From Bayonne in the north-west and Bearn in
the east they came, in pairs, or small groups, or parties of several
score; some laughing, some anxious, some limping, some riding,
many striding out on foot. Whatever their origins or destination,
whether pilgrim, merchant or royal courier, rich or poor, devout or
doubting, for now they were converging on St-Jean-Pied-de-Port, a
bottleneck on the routes across the mountains. And the villages and
towns of this one broad valley fed them, regulated their journeys, and
earned a modest but reliable living from them, in a complex web of
interdependence. Some villages were owned wholly by the great
Orders, the Hospitallers, Premonstratensians or the Augustinians of
Roncevaux. Many were a curious amalgam of lay and religious: a

cluster of houses inhabited by 'donats',[8] some married and some single, all living under the authority of a prior; between them, they shared the tasks of maintaining the chapel fabric and its divine worship, farming the valley fields and woodlands, making cider and a little wine, and running their own small hospitals for the procession of passing pilgrims. None of these lodging places was large, but between them they took in many thousands of pilgrims each year.[9]

At St Palais, Ostabat and St-Jean-Pied-de-Port, the merchants had to pay tolls, on every horse or mule in their train, and on all the gold they carried. Pilgrims, in theory, were exempt, but if you had no safe-conduct, you would certainly have to pay, and even with one you were at the mercy of the officials on duty that day. In this respect even if in no other that Sutton could see, the Basques lived up to the uncivilized reputation so freely given them by the Languedoc French. Grand pilgrims, despite their huge retinues of mounted retainers, might pass unscathed if their safe-conducts were impressive enough, but ordinary folk were not always so fortunate: 'Item from St Paley to Astabat 2 leagues … here you have to pay for 3 pieces of gold which you have by you, under your sworn oath, 2 ordijs and $3\frac{1}{2}$ ordijs as toll for your horse. Item from Astabat to St Johanne de Pede Port, 3 leagues … here you must give … for 3 pieces of gold 2 ordijs, and for your horse as toll 4 ordijs … This seems to be extraordinarily harsh.'[10]

> *And ther men shall make her tribett*
> *For every pice of gold trust me well,*
> *Thou shalt swere upon the Evangele.*[11]

St-Jean-Pied-de-Port, its streets running steeply down to the river and up again on the other side, was the last great meeting point for pilgrims before the mountain pass. Within the sturdy red walls, groups assembled, broke and recombined; people bought food, found cobblers for their footwear, and were cheated and robbed as much or as little as travellers would be in any other town. Those who had come thus far alone, or in twos and threes, attached themselves to larger groups, for despite official royal protection of pilgrims, few would willingly go alone over the mountains, with their wolves, boars and bears, and sudden mists and storms.

Some pilgrims still favoured the old high road to Roncevaux, the Cize road by way of St Michael, Hontto and Chateau Pignon, because it had fewer trees that might shelter beasts of prey, but most preferred to follow the valley road, winding up through the gorges by Arnéguy and Valcarlos. Both routes had hospitals and commanderies of Roncevaux along the way, but the four and a half leagues up the valley offered at least eight places where one could halt for the night if necessary, with four more close by on either side; 14 inns, well-maintained fords and bridges over the worst of the mountain streams. At Valcarlos, the halfway point, there was a castle, a priory of Roncevaux and two good inns, the Capeyron Rouge and the Campana.[12] All this information was very comforting when setting off into the high mountains, up a narrow defile of a valley, hemmed in by forests whose only value seemed to be for fattening pigs on its beech mast, acorns and chestnuts.

As Sutton's party wound their way slowly upwards, hoping to be over the summit before dusk, they could at least tick off these inns and hospitals in their minds, as they passed them one by one, persisting long after the weaker and slower folk gave up and stopped for the night. They could not afford to be over-confident, however; they had all heard enough stories about this particular stage of the journey to know that even the bravest and strongest might be tested to their limits before they reached the top:

> *Then to the Dale of Rouncevale hit is the waie,*
> *A derk passage I der well saie;*
> *Witelez there ben full necessary,*
> *For in that passage my mouth was dry.*[13]

It was not only thirst that gave pilgrims dry mouths that day. The bears and wolves were keeping out of sight among the trees, but their presence was palpable, and overhead in the crisp blue sky the vultures circled lazily, circling and waiting for their next meal. The anxious plodding pilgrims meanwhile grew hotter and hotter, more uncomfortable by the minute, and ever more thirsty, as the road bent and twisted up the widening valley sides. It was a relief at first when the sun went in, and a cool mist veiled its heat, but then real clouds rolled down, and the clear, well-trodden road suddenly became hard to follow. How many prayers then went up to the saints, and how precious the company of other pilgrims suddenly became!

Their pace slowed to an uncertain blundering, the blind leading the blind, encouraging one another on with tales of the old heroes, Charlemagne the Christian King, and his heroes Roland and Olivier. Some garbled, some fanciful, some plain hilarious; wisecracking and soul-stirring tales of battles long ago somehow got their present company up the valley, past even the 'White Horse', the last inn on the road. These places, Valcarlos and, much later and higher up, the chapel at Ibañeta, were redolent of the old legends. There Charles had camped, until he heard his nephew's final horn-blast of despair; here Roland and Olivier had made their last stand and fought their last and greatest battle. Here at Ibañeta Count Roland had died, through Christian treachery, in epic confrontation with the Moors of Spain.

As they stood shivering in the mist on that ancient battlefield at Ibañeta, the clouds rolled dramatically away, and they looked back on their path up the long Valcarlos valley, and the rows of steep mountain sides on either hand. To the right, the road came down to them from the Cize pass; to the left, another group of pilgrims came stumbling down out of the clouds, on another trail over the mountaintops from the west. And here at the summit of the pass, the wind blew suddenly cold on the gathered pilgrims, despite the sun, as they planted little crosses of twigs in the ground as they had been advised to do, on a mound beside the chapel called the Monastery of Charlemagne, and prayed to Our Lady and San Salvador for help at the hour of death.

Half an hour down the far side of the mountain, they came to the great Abbey of Roncevaux, which had been drawing them on and up for so many days. A place dreamed of so ardently it seemed hardly to belong to this world. Under the strong arch, they came into the complex of buildings that seemed to grow directly from the mountain side and from the pilgrim road that crossed it. It grew out of the pilgrim road, but also from the hopes and fears of all who passed its doors and braved the terrors of that road on their journey.

Did the triumph of conquering the mountains carry Sutton on a wave of joy through the days ahead, or did the defeat and human disaster that was also Roncevaux cast him down? Did his delight in Our Lady of Roncevaux outweigh the heavy sadness of seeing other pilgrims carried dead and dying off the mountains, to be laid to rest in the abbey precincts, safe for themselves, but lost to their families who would never know where they lay? Was he fearful of the swifts, devil birds, wheeling and screaming about the high rooftops of the abbey, unnatural creatures that never ceased their flight, never entered the holy precincts? How unlike the swallows, Mary's own dear birds, that appeared at Annunciation and fled again at her Assumption into heaven, and were not afraid to be seen in the monastery courts.

There were many returning pilgrims here, too, who spoke of the dangers ahead: two further mountain ranges, and seemingly endless plains where by midsummer the streams would be running dry. They told him that after all these weeks he was not much more than halfway to Compostela. Could he get there before the festival? If he could not, his safe-conduct from Bordeaux and his new one for Navarre would both have expired long before he could get back. And what then? In many ways, this high point of Roncevaux was also an evening of doubt, a dark night of the soul. After so many challenges, he had achieved this much and it threatened to turn to ashes in his mouth. This place of ancient and legendary defeat was a place for despair, where despite the prayers of holy hermits on the high places of the world, the battle of the pilgrimage was truly joined.

> I beg you, pray you, hear me please,
> You who go to St James.
> Do not hasten on your road,
> But handsomely, gently go.
> For oh! the poor sick pilgrims
> Are struggling and in pain,
> And many who began so bravely
> Will never come home again.[14]

21

Islam and Jewry

… the door was open to all, sick and well, not only Catholics but also pagans, Jews, heretics and vagabonds …[1]

Roncevaux had an anomaly at its heart. This specifically and profoundly Christian institution, set on the salient of the Road to St James, was deeply proud of its open-handed treatment of all suppliants at its doors. Any traveller, whatever their motives, was offered bread by the brother on duty by the gate: the supreme Christian emblem broken and shared freely with all, regardless of nationality, status, sex, race or creed. A symbol of the liberal love of Christ, perhaps, but not the typical response of a militant and crusading Church.

Originally founded in the twelfth century for Compostelan pilgrims, Roncevaux was enlarged and beautified by King Sancho the Strong a few years later, as a thank-offering for his victory over the Moors. Since those early days, the pilgrim routes had been progressively and methodically channelled towards this one pass, until the great majority of pilgrims crossing the Pyrenees came this way. When Sutton and his party got here, the monastery was supplying 25,000 full meals a year, several hundred a day in the busy months. Tons of wheat and barley for bread, waggon-loads of cider and wine, sheep, lambs, goats, pigs and cows, literally hundreds of cheeses each weighing half a stone, almonds and fruit in season, all had to be transported up the mountain roads from the many dependent commanderies, together with sardines without number brought from the distant fishing ports, to feed the resident canons, their staff and their ever-changing quota of guests.[2]

Besides being fed, pilgrims who reached Roncevaux alive were offered a bath, a haircut, the services of a doctor, an apothecary, a cobbler, a tailor, and of course the full round of daily worship in the abbey church. Those who became too ill to get there unaided were carried by horse or mule, or in a waggon, even from the northern borders of Navarre. And for the many who died on the way, especially on the network of tracks over the high mountains, whose bodies were recovered before the wolves and bears and vultures found them, there was burial in the tranquil pilgrim cemetery next to the abbey.

Because of its unique position, the Roncevaux rule allowed pilgrims to stay up to three days instead of the usual two. While they were there, they were shown a whole variety of relics: the tomb of King Sancho, who had stood over two metres tall in life, was presented to them as that of 'Roland the giant'; then they saw Roland and Olivier's hunting horns of ivory, Roland's stirrups, his battle axe and his sword Durendal (all these were actually Sancho's), Archbishop Turpin's slippers, and King Charlemagne's chess board. Having now seen three Oliphants, two tombs of Roland and Olivier and several swords that might have been theirs, Sutton might be forgiven a little scepticism. He probably had more than a suspicion that the ardent promotion and reworking of the Roland legend was serving an ulterior purpose, bolstering the precarious independence and prosperity of the Kingdom of Navarre, perhaps, or serving the ends of the anti-Moslem party that demanded Crusades and the expulsion of the Moors from their last stronghold in southern Spain. To this latter end, St James himself had also been used, in his less familiar guise of Santiago Matamoros, 'St James the Moorslayer'. But there were no Moslem armies anywhere near this pilgrim road to St James and, more surprisingly, the local Basque Christians had always maintained, and still did so most vehemently, that it was they, not the Moors, who had attacked and destroyed Charlemagne's rearguard at Roncevaux. The ideal of a Christian warrior king fighting a just war fitted comfortably into Sutton's world-view; this after all was what Henry V had epitomized so brilliantly. But some of the stories about Roland did not quite add up.

As Sutton left Roncevaux behind him and turned westwards down into the steeply rolling Navarrese countryside, he could not help noticing another very odd fact. For Navarre, although a Christian kingdom, was a multi-racial, multi-faith society. There were Jewish and Moslem craftsmen and artisans of all kinds, and sick pilgrims soon discovered that many of the best doctors were Jewish too. Christian labourers were sometimes paid a bonus, but usually no distinction was made between the faiths. The only real difference seemed to be that Moorish women did not engage in heavy manual work. Their menfolk, by contrast, were happy to work as labourers, bricklayers and stonemasons, and so by a curious twist of fate they were responsible for building and repairing some of the finest churches on the pilgrim road.

At Pamplona, two days on from Roncevaux, the diverse nature of the society that Sutton was now moving in was thrown still further into relief. For the first time in his life, he found himself in a city with a thriving and respected Jewish population. Worcester, and all the other big English cities he knew of, had once had a Jewish quarter, but England and France alike had expelled their Jews generations ago. Navarre not only included Jews, it welcomed them and, since the accession of Charles III, actively protected them.

Pamplona itself was a strange city, in three parts. The old city, up on a steep hill above the River Arga, was approached over a long bridge and through heavily fortified ramparts. It contained the cathedral, royal palace, castle and a large Jewish quarter set within its own internal palisade. Beyond, and separated from this walled city by a narrow space, were two further walled settlements, the San Cernin and San Nicholas districts. The churches of St James, St Francis and St Eulalie were distributed around the outside of these subsidiary areas.[3]

For Sutton, the free acceptance of the Jews of Pamplona, their freedom to mix with their Christian and Moslem neighbours, was a radical, new and deeply unsettling concept. It was especially hard to comprehend in a divided city infamous for its riots between the Basques, French and other Christian communities that made up the bulk of the population. These Jews were, after all, the hereditary enemies of Christendom, traditionally singled out for attack when disaster struck. Yet here in the cities of Navarre, they were living under the express patronage of the King, not confined to the ghetto near their synagogue, but many of them choosing to live in other places that suited them better. In Pamplona, they ran the main abbatoir, and so controlled much of the butchery and leather trades, including supplying meat and skins to the royal court. They worked as tailors, hosiers, weavers, furriers, curtain and hanging-makers, and the richest of them were merchants, dealing particularly in the staples of wine, fruit and grain, and trading with the Biscay ports for sardines and other fish.[4] Only the lucrative pork trade was beyond the orbit of the Jews, despite its key role in the Navarrese economy:

> *Sardyns and bacon shall fynde the Spanyard and me,*
> *Wyth suche meate we be contente in all our countre.*[5]

Through all their trade and creativity, the Jews had two great advantages denied to Christians. There was no religious impediment to their studying the new ideas in medicine introduced to Spain by the Moors, so many of them became highly successful and eminent doctors. In Pamplona they even ran a medical hospital. And they were permitted to deal in money, veiling their usury for the benefit of tender Christian consciences with delicate turns of phrase such as 'bills of obligation'. The Jewish dealers and money-lenders exchanged internationally accepted florins for the doubtful new Navarrese coinage, made loans to their Christian neighbours, and generally made themselves very useful.

Besides being the capital city of Navarre, Pamplona had a special interest for Robert Sutton, for one of the kingdom's major imports was fine English cloth, much of it shipped from Bristol to Bordeaux and then transported overland on the very roads he had himself walked in the last two weeks. If Bordeaux had stirred memories of home, he would have been a strange man not to be intrigued and a little curious to see the Navarrese nobility and the wealthier Pamplona citizens wearing clothes that might have been dyed in his own workshop far away on Eport Street. The aristocracy of Navarre loved the rich Bristol colours: plain red 'rojo', a vermilion 'bermejo', and a vivid madder-dyed 'granza', but they also bought murrey, azure, perse-blue, violet, turquoise, grey, scarlet, white, an increasingly fashionable range of greens, and burnets and blacks for mourning clothes. So popular were the English greens, the colour of love, that Sutton could be reasonably confident that any fine green cloth he saw on the streets of Pamplona was English, and had probably been exported from Bristol. The local Navarrese wool, inferior in every way, was used by the lower classes and for white linings.[6]

Sutton was now in a city so eager to promote the pilgrimage to Compostela that he found he had special guarantees and security for his person and possessions. At a time when neighbouring Castile had been growing more powerful and steadily more aggressive, tiny landlocked Navarre depended on keeping her trade routes open, including the pilgrim road.[7] If the pilgrims and merchants lost confidence in the nation's ability or desire to protect them, they would find other thoroughfares and other outlets, and Navarre, caught between larger and wealthier rivals, would be crushed like a peppercorn in a mortar. So Pamplona made sure it offered pilgrims plenty of accommodation, with good food and attentive staff, so that even the most demanding were satisfied: 'In the town they give free wine and food to twelve pilgrims every day. Do not forget that on the left is the Hospital of Our Lady; there they will give willingly for the sake of God. You should be glad of this.'[8]

Navarre, where the court spoke French and Latin and the bulk of the population spoke Basque, had to be realistic about the international nature of the pilgrimage. In a Holy Year such as this, general safe-conducts were proclaimed by the court, stressing the need to honour those who passed through the country: 'the inhabitants of the kingdoms of Italy, France, Germany, Hungary, Denmark, Sweden, Norway and all other nations, ... by land, by sea, by day and by night'.[9] Some of these foreigners, especially the ever-curious Germans, were intrigued by the mysterious Basque language, unlike any other they had met on their travels, and made an attempt to learn a few key phrases (their choice revealing much about their interests): 'Item in Pascayen they have their own language which is difficult to write, but I have retained some words which are written below – bread, water, meat, cheese, salt, oats, straw, who is there?, how much is that?, inkeeper, ... Beautiful maiden come and sleep with me ...'[10]

Occasionally as they travelled, some nationalities gravitated towards particular hospitals where they knew they would be better understood; the Italian Order of Santiago de Altopascio ran a house in Pamplona where Italian speakers felt especially at home. And sometimes one national group found a particular focus for their devotion, like the life-size crucifix at Puenta la Reina, one day farther down the road, which had been carried there by a party of German pilgrims; perhaps they were holy penitents, or perhaps they were fulfilling a state-imposed public penance, but the dedication required to carry this massive tree of sacrifice all the way to the heart of Navarre touched the souls of all who saw it, and none more so than their German compatriots.[11]

However for most pilgrims, most of the time, the journey had long since become an experience where national identity faded away; a long perspective, terrifying at times, often quite interesting, with daily needs reduced to the bare essentials, a clear routine that fitted ever more closely with one's fellow travellers, and a skill in making oneself understood in sign language and polyglot that would have seemed astonishing three months earlier.

22
The War-torn Border

Then to the Gruon in Spayne,
That is the last toune, certaine,
Of the realme of Naveron;
. . . A gud contraie, and evell wyn,
And witelez ther ben bothe gud and fyn.[1]

After Puenta la Reina, there was a change of pace and a distinct change of atmosphere. No sooner had the gentle securities of peaceful, pastoral, mountain-cradled central Navarre lulled the senses, than they began to be insidiously replaced by a more arid landscape and a remorseless series of hills to be toiled up and staggered down, under an ever more unforgiving sun.

From Estella, where there were relics of St Bartholomew, the Holy Innocents and the True Cross,[2] to Los Arcos, the sun was at its zenith for midsummer. The increasing heat began to make itself felt, in discomfort on the road, storms threatening by mid-afternoon, and a sense of unease in the cities at night. Estella's mixed population of Jews, Basques and Languedoc French lived in constant simmering discontent and petty feuding; at Los Arcos, the heavens turned black as Sutton's party came in through newly completed town walls: thunder bounced off the ring of surrounding hills, stabs of lightning streaked the sky, and huge drops of rain were swallowed up by the thirsty dust of the road.

Here in the west, Navarre was not such a happy land. An underlying sense of calamity was in the air, coupled with a lingering fear of neighbouring Castile. Even Pamplona itself had been besieged 50 years earlier, and Estella and a score of other castles were temporarily ceded to the enemy in the 'peace' that had been forced on them. Now Castile in turn seemed to be becoming weaker, and Los Arcos had fortified itself against further military aggression. But nothing could defend the country against successive assaults of drought, flood, plague and summer hailstorms, nor guard against the two decades of stagnation that had resulted. Then, just when things were beginning to look up, three hard winters had combined with fearsome summer storms to reduce the people's resistance, so when the plague returned with a vengeance in autumn 1421, victims were easy to find. For over a year pestilence had raged, leaving some villages with only a handful of old women and tiny children alive, and decimating the population of Estella.[3]

One bright spot in this otherwise depressing scene was that many food items were much cheaper for Sutton than they might otherwise have been, and people were desperately keen to benefit from the pilgrim trade. Red wine was a third the price it had been four years earlier, and pears, peas, rice, figs, dates and cheese were all readily available. Some aspects of the local diet were very strange: sardines and herrings entirely replaced cod at the fast-day table; a pound of almonds could be bought for the same price as one skinny rabbit, and a full carapito measure of

wine, enough for a dozen thirsty men, cost the same as two pounds of
cheese.[4] Anything that could be picked from fruit trees, or harvested
from existing vineyards, or raised and sold quickly, like eggs and the
ubiquitous Navarrese pigs, represented income for the surviving
people, and food for the river of pilgrims that flowed past their doors.

Not all travellers were pilgrims, of course, and not all the pilgrims
elected to complete their journeys. More than a few of the inhabitants
of the towns strung out along the roads through Navarre had set out
from distant places fully intending to go to Compostela, but had chosen
not to return home. For some, the journey simply proved too arduous;
they became ill or lost the will to persist, or fell for a pretty face at a
small Spanish inn, and gave up before they even reached Castile. Others
completed their outward pilgrimage and then, with sins forgiven,
indulgences gained and slate wiped clean, settled down in one of the
pleasant towns they had spied out as they went along. There they found
land to spare, work to be done and a living to be made. For some it
might have been a spur-of-the-moment decision; others no doubt were
consciously escaping difficult situations, bad debts or unhappy
marriages at home. Many brought their skills and trades to the
economy of the pilgrim roads. They worked as cobblers, tapsters,
innkeepers or tailors, or bought small farms, or went into service at the
big monasteries and hospitals. A few deliberately chose to devote the
rest of their lives to the pilgrims, and themselves became part of the
miracle of the pilgrimage, submerging their identities in the ranks of
the 'servants of Christ's poor'.

Of all these little towns in western Navarre, only Viana was
conspicuously military in origin. All the others seemed to be more or
less arranged along the pilgrim road, depending on it for their survival
and seeming to have grown up just because the pilgrims were there.
Only Viana was different, scowling out towards Castile across the
ravine-cracked plains, a tiny Navarrese David on its craggy hill, defying
the imperial Goliath beyond. Having fallen to Castile in 1378 and since
been returned to Navarre, the town was elevated in 1423 to the status
of a royal fief and principality for the heir to the throne, a calculated
snub and a courageous gesture of Davidic defiance, taunting an old
enemy growing impotent with troubles of its own.

For Sutton, the main effect of these rumblings in the borderlands was that frontier towns were more heavily garrisoned, and tolls were more likely to be exacted. There was no payment demanded on leaving Navarre, but at the great 12-arched stone bridge over the mighty River Ebro,[5] the gateway to Logroño and the kingdom of Castile, money had to be changed into the Spanish currency of maravedise and groats, and a tribute paid to the royal exchequer, whether you were merchant or pilgrim:

> *Jakkez ben ther of little prise,*
> *For there beginneth the Marvedisez …*
> *And from thennez to Grunneole,*
> *Much pyn men ther thoole [suffer]*
> *Hit ston upon a hull on hyy,*
> *And Jewez ben lordez of all that countray.*
> *Ther most thou tribute make, or thou passe,*
> *For alle thi gud bothe mor and lasse;*
> *Of that tribute they be full fayne,*
> *For thei hyeer hit of the King of Spayn.*[6]

PART VIII

Camino across Castile

23

The Way of St James

Here wyn is theke as any blode,
And that wuld make men wode.
Bedding ther is nothing faire,
Mony pilgrimez hit doth apaire [pain].
Tabelez use thei non of to ete,
But on the bare flore they make her sete;[1]

There was little danger of getting lost on the long *camino* across
Castile. All Sutton had to do was to raise his eyes from the road, and
see the stream of travellers, flowing in both directions, snaking up
and down the land ahead. There was often a choice of paths, but all
were well used and all fed back into the main river of humanity
before long. Each day, the road was easy enough to follow, but in the
mind's eye the sequence of events soon became confused: so many
hospitals, so many shrines, each memorable in some way, but mostly
fading and blending into each other like the shimmering heat haze
on the crest of every hill.

Some places did stand out, for one reason or another. On the
evening of St John the Baptist, Sutton and a group of other pilgrims
came into Santo Domingo de la Calzada, St Dominic of the
Causeway, a neat little city chiefly memorable for the rock-cut tomb
of the saint, and the white cockerel in the cathedral, which crowed
throughout Mass next day. This cockerel and a white hen were kept
in a cage there in memory of a miracle that they were told had
happened there many years ago, by the intervention of St James. A

138

young man and his parents were passing through on their pilgrimage when the innkeeper's daughter became so enraged that the youth would not submit to her advances that she hid a silver cup in his bag, and had him hanged for theft. His parents continued sadly on their way and, returning several weeks later, were amazed to find their son still alive on the gibbet:

> 'Do not be sorrowful, for . . . since you went away a good man has supported me so I have come to no harm.' So they hurried to the judge to ask him to fetch their son down from the gibbet, because he was alive . . . and the judge did not believe it, for it was impossible . . . and the judge had a cock and hen roasting on a spit for his dinner . . . and he said it was just as likely that they would come off the spit and sing as that the boy could be alive. And they came off the spit and sang . . . And ever after, in that church, they have kept a cock and a hen . . . and I have seen them, and they are pure white.[2]

Burgos, the capital of Castile, also left a powerful impression. Its Augustinian monastery housed the miraculous Santo Cristo crucifix,

> made neither of wood nor stone . . . Its hair and nails grow . . . and when one grasps the skin it feels like a man's. It has a dreadful and solemn countenance. Great masters say that Nicodemus prayed to God as he took him down from the Cross that he would suffer him to make a likeness of him as he was crucified. That night the cucifix appeared to him. It remained for a long time in his charge . . . On the day when we saw the crucifix, two great miracles occurred [or perhaps three?]. A child who had been dead three days, a child with two broken legs and a man that had the wild fire were all made well . . . [3]

Burgos was much the largest city for many leagues around. It was full of wool traders bringing in the new clip, merchants, dealers and muleteers preparing their trains for the journey to the ports, and over thirty hospitals catering for the great concourse of pilgrims who nightly gathered there. Those who had a day's rest at Burgos, and were well informed, spent their second night outside the city, at the magnificent King's Hospital. Out through the red San Martín gate, down the hill through the suburbs and over the bridge, it was comfortable and convenient whether or not pilgrims wished to indulge in some ghoulish sightseeing while they were there: 'The King's Hospital is the best of all; they give you plenty to eat and drink. Do not overlook the Hospital of the Little Hen; they have good beds and give food and drink. You can also go to the Knight's Hospital. Many pilgrims will want to see the pillar at which the hospital master who poisoned four hundred and fifty pilgrims was put to death. If you cross the bridge on the right it is near the King's Hospital.'[4]

From Burgos to Castrojeríz was a long hard day for the Feast of St Peter and St Paul, another day with moments etched in the mind as sharply as the shadows in the sun. From the comfort and cacophony of Burgos, out across the long arid plains, it was late afternoon before they came down into a wooded valley between steep limestone scarps, to the San Antón Convent, a monumental Antonine hospital whose arches spanned the road so loftily that their detail was lost in the shadows. The familiar Tau cross emblazoned in the windows and the bread and wine set ready for them in the hatch beneath the arch, where they gathered in the welcoming shade to rest, were signs and gifts from heaven. Then, doggedly on the road again, it wasn't long before their eyes were drawn to the strange conical hill of Castrojeríz far ahead, but distances were deceptive on these shimmering plains, and it was a full hour before the little hill grew into a great summit, crowned by a fortress, with the convent of St Mary of the Apples at its feet, and the town and its hospitals nestling on its flank.

Mansilla de las Mulas, the city of the mule fairs, was reached on the evening of St Martin of Tours, the pilgrims coming wearily in through the Santa María gate in the high walls to the church of San Martín[5] just as dusk fell, and struggling to stay awake for vespers for the saint. And so, the next day, a short journey brought them to León, once a splendid capital city, now sidelined by the unification of the two kingdoms, and more concerned with pilgrims than politics.[6] Making their way up through the outer walled city, past numerous churches and hospitals, they penetrated the inner city, within a second ring of walls, and came to the cathedral, where they joined a queue of other pilgrims, waiting to touch the twin pillars of St James the Pilgrim and Our Lady the Fair and give thanks for another round of dangers passed.[7]

Our Lady's shrines so dominated and shaped this *camino* across Castile that Sutton's road became a living rosary to her name. At Logroño and Nájera, Burgos, La Virgen de Villalcazar, Carrión de los Condes, La Peregrina at Sahagún, and now León, time and again he found shrines and wonder-working statues, and countless monasteries in her honour. The Holy Virgin was no longer a saint to be sought out and implored for help. She was travelling with them on their journey, as constant and familiar a companion as their own humble wooden rosaries. She was the Virgen Peregrina, who had experienced the discomforts of travel in foreign lands for herself, and who appeared visibly and actively in times of danger. At Carrión she had defeated the Moors when they demanded tribute, at Villalcazar her cult was so strong that many pilgrims in the past had felt no need to look further for absolution, and as Our Lady of the Market Place in León she protected the grain market of the city as well as exercising her patronage of the road. Even her ancient visitors the Three Kings had come to be seen as fellow pilgrims, carrying walking staves as they journeyed to find the Christ Child.

These holy helpers were all the more necessary since these hot, high tablelands were proving to be a surprisingly hard trial. Despite the labours of men like Santo Domingo and his disciple San Juan, who had given practical expression to their faith by building bridges across streams and rivers, and causeways across uneven and treacherous ground, despite all the faithful service of the hospitals and monasteries, this was still a dangerous road. The food was unfamiliar, the heat intense and unrelenting; clothes that had been inadequate in the northern spring were now oppressively hot, feet still swathed in boots now sweltered, and the heavy local wine and infrequent fountains and streams made thirst a constant torment. No wonder hell was portrayed as a region of eternal fire. The grain was standing ready for harvest, but death lurked by the road in many guises. Wolves patrolled in the woods, waiting for an easy meal; vultures and ravens quartered the sky.

Through this interminable trek, the fellowship of the bands of pilgrims became a precious bond of solidarity. Tales were told of men who carried their dying companions with them until their strength failed, to be rescued at length by a majestic knight on a white horse, who bore them both off to Compostela in the blink of an eye. There were also stories of pilgrims driven crazy by thirst, tormented by visions from hell until they were willing to sell their souls for a drink, but saved by the intervention of a bearded Pilgrim who showed them a hidden fountain and brought them water in a scallop shell.

But everyone nursed some fear in his heart, because for every miraculous intervention, a hundred pilgrims might die by the wayside, of hunger, of thirst, of diseases carried from home or caught on the road, poisoned by strange food or set upon by robbers and left for dead. It was well said, in the French proverb: 'Pelerin qui chante, Larron épouvante',[8] but they could be forgiven if some of their songs had a melancholy note.

And who were they, these pilgrims that Sutton travelled with across the broiling tablelands of Castile? Through sifting and sorting, companies of like-minded travellers slowly took shape, travelling each at their own pace. The most miserable struggled slowly on, making only a few leagues a day, seeking charity where they could, or huddled helpless by the roadside, taking it in turn to keep watch for wolves. Anyone joining these most destitute bands must accept the pace at which they travelled and the conditions in which they lived, not least the fleas and lice that they repeatedly picked from their clothes. 'Whan thei wer wyth-owtyn the townys, hir felaschepe [companions] dedyn of her clothys, &, sittyng nakyd, pykyd hem . . . Thys creatur was a-bauyd [afraid] to putte of hir clothis as hyr felawys dedyn, & therfor she . . . had part of her vermyn & was betyn & stongyn ful evyl bothe day & nyght'.[9]

At the other end of the social spectrum, there were plenty of wealthy pilgrims who overtook Sutton on the road, travelling with private entourages, armed escorts, brightly caparisoned horses, mule trains of provisions and saddle bags laden with personal effects. Bishops, the nobility, envoys, ambassadors and pleasure-seeking adventurers, they could travel swiftly if they chose, and might complete the journey to Compostela and back before their personal 40-day safe-conducts from the king of Navarre expired.[10]

Between these two extremes, there was a widely varied assortment of pilgrims, more or less compatible with Sutton but drawn from many walks of life and all the nations of Europe. Some had been on foot all the way, others had begun mounted but had abandoned their horses and were now reduced to ambling mules or their own two feet. Horses were at a premium in Castile, and fodder was hard to come by, so many were eventually left behind in the hope of retrieving them on the return journey. There were also strict customs regulations, forcing some pilgrims to leave their mounts on the border, where 'for your horse you pay two reals as duty and you must take a letter with you that you have brought such a horse, of such appearance and size, with you into the country. Otherwise when you want to leave the country again, by whatever exit, they will take your horse as stolen or purchased. For this reason one has to pay this heavy duty.'[11]

Among the pilgrims to Compostela was a young grocer who had travelled down from the Baltic coast with his manservant, combining the pilgrimage with a business trip to make contacts for trade in France and the Spanish kingdoms. He hoped to go home with enough prestige to make a good marriage and achieve entry into the ruling classes of his city, despite his humble origins.[12] A pair of cheerful Genoese Franciscans had walked through Provence to Toulouse (where the church of St Sernin claimed, in defiance of Compostela, to house the body of St James) before skirting the mountain foothills to Ostabat and Roncevaux.[13] A pious English gentlewoman with her serving man and maid, who had already visited many of the greatest shrines of Christendom, was glad to have joined a respectable group that included English speakers.[14] A Flemish cloth merchant and his servant, a Bohemian couple, two Poles and three citizens of Bayonne coming back from the shrine of St Eulalie at Barcelona, had all been travelling together since Puenta la Reina. To their number had been added a man who astonished and alarmed all who saw him: an Eastern Christian so dark of complexion that his safe-conduct from the king of Aragon specifically forbade anyone to mistreat him on that account.[15]

All these had become knit into a group, accompanied by several humbler pilgrims carrying musical instruments of various kinds, who were welcomed for their contribution to the morale of the company.

Nobody wanted to delay unnecessarily, but neither did anyone have the means or need to make undue haste. As they walked, they sang. Each nation taught its own songs to the others, secular and religious alike, and added new words to suit their mood. They sang loudly as they crossed the rough country of the Montes de Oca, to scorn their fears and warn off brigands. For inspiration through the long midday, they sang rousing marching songs to the beat of a little pipe and tabor, and they sang cheerful songs of triumph each evening, accompanied by hurdy-gurdy, fiddel and shawm, as they came in sight of their next place of rest.

> *Dum Paterfamilias, Rex universorum,*
> *Donaret provincias jus Apostolorum,*
> *Jacobus Hispanias lux illustrat morum.*

> **Primus ex Apostolis! Martyr Jerosolimis!*
> *Jacobus Egregio sacer est martyrio.*

> *Jacobi Gallecia open rogat piam,*
> *Glebe cuius gloria dat insignem viam,*
> *Ut precum frequentia cantet melodiam:*
> *Herru Sanctiagu! Got Sanctiagu!*
> *E Ultreia! E sus eia! Deus adjuva nos.*[16]

24
Mountains and Miracles

If you want to go to Astorga you cross three bridges and go up a hill where there is a large stone cross at which you turn left for Astorga. But if you follow my advice turn to the right here and you will not have to climb the mountains as they all lie on the left. My advice is to avoid Rabanal.[1]

In two weeks, they could be in Compostela. The long-desired goal was almost within their grasp, separated from them by two mountain ranges, one reputedly arid and hot, the other mist-shrouded and muddy. Here the varied motivations of the pilgrims were thrown into stark relief. Sutton, and the others in his group, had their eyes firmly fixed on St James, reaching out across the pilgrimage to grasp their hands and draw them on. Other groups, less fervent or perhaps less fit, chose to turn north here, opting for a lower, longer path. For even if these mountains were not as dramatic as some had encountered in Switzerland, they still demanded respect, and they claimed many lives at the very portals of the Apostle.

Some groups elected to make a different diversion at León, bearing right for the city of Oviedo; but this was less for the ease of their bodies than for the good of their souls. For there 'two pottez may thou se, In the wiche water turnet to vyn'.[2] Many pilgrims felt it was well worth a four-day deviation from their direct route to see the water jars in which Christ performed his first miracle at Cana in Galilee, a miracle told and retold in stories and plays all over Christendom. Oviedo was peculiarly well-endowed with relics of all kinds to amaze and awe the faithful: a portion of the True Cross, several thorns from Christ's crown, the swaddling clothes, part of the manger, some manna and a piece of the bread from the Last Supper;

then there was the hand of St Stephen, hair of Mary Magdalene, the baskets used by Peter and Andrew at the feeding of the five thousand (with some grilled fish) and one of the coins with which Judas was paid for the Betrayal. Such a spiritual treasure-trove, even leaving aside some of its less plausible elements, was enough to tempt many from the shortest way. But having come so far, and being now so close to Compostela that the city and its loveliness was still crystal clear in the minds of the homeward-bound travellers they met, it seemed better to Sutton's group to press on over the mountains, and hope to see the miraculous water jars of Oviedo on the way back.

Leaving León on the day after the Feast of Thomas Becket (one of whose hair shirts they were told could be seen at Compostela), they came after two days to Astorga, secure behind its old ramparts on top of its hill. Entering the city through the eastern Puerta del Sol, Sutton's party was confronted at once with a bewildering choice of hospitals to try: San Martín, San Francisco, San Juan and a score of others, while out in the suburbs the hospital of Thomas Becket was a reminder (if one were needed) that they were still in the octave of England's premier pilgrimage saint, whose shrine at Canterbury many of the assembled crowd had already visited. Astorga's Frankish quarter and even larger Jewish quarter vied with each other for the lucrative pilgrim trade in jostling noisy contention, as a further flood of pilgrims came in on their own roads up from the south. Despite the thronging masses, it was surprisingly easy to find food and get minor repairs made to footwear in preparation for the mountains. Long experience had groomed Astorga for its task, and even if it had been a Sunday the cobblers would have been permitted to work for pilgrims in need.

From Astorga, the mountains of Rabanal were already visible; not menacing, but inviting caution. Slowly and steadily, the road ascended through heathland and heather, past a series of hospitals and the Premonstratensian monastery at El Ganso, until the fields became more stone than soil, and the oak trees grew so stunted and gnarled one expected to be able to see over their crowns. All day they climbed into the uplands, a wide rolling landscape of broad valleys and hills. Then, as the sheep and goats were being led in for the night, they came into the village of Rabanal; warm yellow stones, caring staff at the hospice on the left, and in the middle of the village the old Templar church of Santa María. The Templars were long-since gone, disgraced and their lands reallocated, but the tradition of protection of pilgrims in Rabanal lived on. Here, far up on the hillside, in a village created for the pilgrimage but supporting a life of its own, they rested for the night.

Snow had been falling on these mountains in early June, and the night air struck chill after the heat of the day. But next morning it was warm again, becoming uncomfortably hot as they trudged up the winding mountain road to the pass at Foncebadón. The road here was clearly marked with tall posts, visible, so the innkeeper assured them, in even the deepest snow. It was part of the privileges of the neighbouring hospice to keep it so.

Along the whale-backed summit of the pass, more hospitals had disgorged their overnight guests, and the staff were going about the business of the day. Then at the bigger village of Manjarín the road began to descend, gradually at first but soon more sharply, past the little town of El Acebo, the grey brother of Rabanal, down a twisting valley full of white and blood-red cistus that spoke of the Passion, and banks of yellow genistas and startling wild lavender.

Like a restless night ended, the road turned a corner and they were down off the mountains. The highlands of Rabanal were suddenly over. The village itself had proved to be a small miracle in the mountains, and down in the valley near a youthful river they stopped by common consent for a well-earned Sunday night.

Pressing on next day, hourly more eager to reach journey's end, they came into the town of Ponferrada over a grand stone bridge. But pausing only to comment on the disproportionate bulk of the castle, even then being enlarged still further, they soon left the city behind them and entered a hilly region of fertile farmland, frequent hospitals and rich strong wine that could 'burn up a man's heart so that he goes out like a candle'.[3] Fortunately for the northern palates in the party, although ale could not be found for love nor money, there were now many apple orchards to be seen, and there was gentle cider to slake their thirst.

At Villafranca del Bierzo, where they halted for another night, the landscape changed again. Behind were the low-lying hills; ahead, the land rose up in fold after fold, higher and still higher, with no summit in sight. Villafranca had a reputation for generosity to pilgrims whose hearts failed them at this last great barrier on their road. A castle kept brigands in check, and the tolls that were once demanded had long since been abolished. As a consequence, the Cluniac church of Santa María, once a proud beneficiary of these unjust levies, was reduced to penurious ruin.[4] But there were still five other hospitals flourishing; Santiago, which greeted travellers from the east as they first entered the town, not surprisingly drew in those ailing ones who felt they could go no further. They struggled as far as the north door of the church, and appealed to the gentle-faced Christ for mercy. Then they were taken into the hospital, to recover or to die, to make one last push for Compostela, or to rest for ever at Villafranca.[5]

For Sutton, intent on completing his pilgrimage to St James, Villafranca had a different meaning. It was a stepping-stone into the final mountains. And so the party set off again, up the valley, pacing their progress to each other's needs, some slower up the steepest parts, some more cautious crossing the frequent streams. As they went up higher, the valley narrowed and it began to drizzle. Wet and muddy, dripped on by interminable oak and pine woods, through towns and villages, still they ascended, past hospitals large and small, until suddenly they were so high they were walking in the very clouds, their sodden clothes clinging to their limbs, feet slipping at every step.

After what seemed an age of uncertain progress, a shape loomed close beside their path. There was no time even to be afraid, before they heard a human voice, unintelligible but warm, inviting and friendly, and then, repeated like a holy incantation, the name of 'O Cebreiro'. They remembered that place for ever, as a warm thatched roof over their heads, devoted French monks, dry beds, and a table laden with rye bread, cheese, bacon and soup. It was a miracle on the mountain tops.

The church there held a wonder of its own, a chalice in which the daily miracle of the Mass had been fulfilled in all its glory. A doubting and grudging priest, resenting his duty to celebrate in a blizzard for one faithful peasant, had seen the wine changed and moving before his own eyes, barely a hundred years before.

Whatever it was he had seen, he had never doubted again, and the chalice he had used that winter's day was preserved for all to see in the church. Mass in the morning at O Cebreiro was a close encounter with the divine, transfigured high on the mountain.

After that it was downhill, winding down into rolling, verdant, well-farmed Galicia, sun-blessed and rain-washed, ruled by Castile but strangely like the England that Sutton knew. Oak woods, rich meadows, full streams, frequent rain, and mud. When the sun came out, the pilgrims sang with the crickets; when it rained, they slithered along, and sang anyway. At Triacastela they squeezed into a small hospice, at Sarría they chose the larger one of El Salvador, up above the rapidly expanding new town. At Portomarín they rested with the Hospitallers, and then made a short Saturday's journey as far as Ligonde, to the Hospital of the Order of the Knights of Saint James.

One more day and they were at Melide, in the well-appointed new Franciscan hospice of the Holy Spirit, 'furnished with all the linen needed to receive and shelter the poor and impoverished pilgrims who need help', with 12 large beds in its generous dormitory.[6] Other groups of pilgrims soon filled every last space, here and at the older hospitals in the town, at San Pedro and Santa María de Melli. Some of these folk had come down on the road from Oviedo, and were full of the wonders they had seen there, the miraculously preserved bread from the Last Supper, and the pots that had held water turned into wine. But Sutton had climbed the road to O Cebreiro, and his companions had stood with him in a church on a mountaintop, where they believed they had seen a cup that had held the living, pulsing Blood of Christ. That was his miracle.

Whether from Oviedo or O Cebreiro, the river of pilgrims now marched in triumphant expectation over the last leagues to St James. Every few minutes it seemed that they passed another house offering accommodation, or food, so the great numbers were catered for all along the road. There were also frequent sly hawkers here, more numerous than on previous days, offering them scallop tokens they swore were as valid as the more expensive ones sold in Compostela, and ivory carvings of St James that looked as if they were pig bone, and many other doubtful trinkets that the pilgrims passed by with scorn.

One more night, and the next day they would be in Compostela. But where to spend that night, with the press on the road becoming hourly more urgent as the day of the festival approached? Fearful of missing the chance of finding a bed, they stopped much earlier than they might have done, at a little Antonine house by a gurgling stream, easily fordable but, in the compassionate way of the *camino*, crossed here by a stout stone bridge. The valley was lush and green, the hospital clearing set among mixed woodland, with contented sheep cropping the damp turf. The Antonines had been an unexpected source of strength to Sutton on his pilgrimage, ever since he first spent a night in their care way back in Poitou for Pentecost. In the Landes of Gascony, at Castrojeríz and now in Galicia, their houses had been there when he needed them, for nursing care, for refreshment in the heat of the day, or for a good night's rest. Here at Ribadiso, one day short of his journey's end, he had found them again and they welcomed him with open arms.[7]

They had a long march to make next day, but it was worth it to be starting off from such a haven, meeting people in the early morning light emerging damply from beside village hayricks, from under barn eaves or church porches, anywhere they had found to rest for a few hours overnight once the groaning hospital beds had squeezed in their last occupants. So with heads held high, they sang their repertoire of songs through one more time: German songs with new Italian words, a haunting Indian tune with a trilingual chorus, songs they all knew and sang in unison, each in their own language. Thus Sutton and his band of companions made their last march to Compostela. He thought they would never get there, but he did not want the day to end.

When afternoon was far advanced, they came down into a little valley of red earth, and joined a dozen other parties of pilgrims by the meandering stream. They washed their faces and hands, they washed their feet, and they washed as much more as they chose to or dared. Then, clean and refreshed and suddenly solemn, they made their way up the long gradual ascent of the heathy hill, on and up for what seemed like an age, until all at once a great shout of triumph ahead told them they were there, at the top of Mount Joy.

Up there, beside the cairn of stones and the great cross, Sutton and a hundred other pilgrims like him took off their hats, and stared in reverent awe at Compostela, city of their longing, etched in the evening light in the valley below. The vespers breeze ruffling their hair, choking with emotion and blinded by sudden tears, they sang a *Te Deum* of fervent gratitude. Then in the last light of day Sutton took off his boots and walked barefoot down the hill to St James's city.

25
Journey's End?

And then to Sent Jamez that holy place;
There maie thou fynde full faire grace.[1]

Early next morning, they joined the crowd of new arrivals making their way from the numerous hospitals and inns along the Rua Francigena to the cathedral. The streets were paved with great slabs of stone, and washed clean by the overnight rain. Already the shops and money-changers' booths lining the road were open and doing brisk business, but it wasn't until they came to the square called the Paradise, next to the cathedral, that the full scale of Compostela's commercial commitment to the pilgrimage became clear. The square, a stone's throw across, was seething with stalls selling everything that could possibly tempt a pilgrim's eye: scrips, belts, flagons and shoes, fine goatskin boots and thick-soled wooden pattens and clogs, scallops, badges and medicines of every kind for every conceivable ailment.

Leaving this hubbub behind for the time being, they became part of a procession of pilgrims snaking round the cathedral, and climbed the long flight of steps to the west front, where St James sat, patiently waiting for them at the feet of Christ. Behind his head there was a scallop shell halo, and his bare feet, strong walking staff and gentle endurance showed them he understood their pilgrimage. There was no need to hurry; go steadily, faithfully on your way and see, you have reached journey's end. In the moment of embracing the pillar on which he sat, saint and suppliant were united, and tears flowed.

This, then, was journey's end for the group of companions that Sutton had grown to love and trust so well. The Franciscans had already left them, spirited away to their own convent the evening before. Most of the remainder stayed together until they were back in the noisy square, and entered the lesser noise of the cathedral. But there they were divided, according to nationality and language. Castilians and Latin speakers went one way, the others were led into a large chapel, almost a separate church, where they were parcelled out among a team of translators. Sutton's man was friendly, business-like but kind, a Benedictine happy to be living here in Spain. He heard his confession, inspected his bundle of documents from Worcester and those picked up along the way, at Southampton, Bordeaux and in Navarre, noted with approval the badges from Wilton, Saintes and Santo Domingo, and clucked in ready sympathy that Sutton had failed to visit Mont St Michel. Finally, he made out a certificate on behalf of the 'Cardinals and Treasurer of the Cathedral of St James', sealed with the insignia of the altar of the Apostle, so all who saw it would know that he, Robert Sutton, had 'well and fully completed his pilgrimage'.[2]

Journey's end for a personal pilgrimage back towards grace. Shriven, armed with his certificate, and now standing in the cathedral nave for Mass, surrounded by so many other pilgrims, all at their own private goals, unknown by face but brothers in experience, Sutton had reached the end of his penitential road.

And yet it was not journey's end at all. Four days remained before the festival itself. Four days in which to change money into silver coin for a cathedral offering, and to buy new clothes for the journey home. The poorest and most threadbare pilgrims were given new clothes without charge; for the others, the city tailors and cordwainers were kept fully employed. All pilgrims could be found free board and lodging if needed, but Sutton had, by the grace of

God and the protection of St James, escaped mishap on his journey, and could pay for everything he required.

He bought a fine pewter scallop shell badge from one of the hundred official stalls, a badge with St James embossed on it, with his scallop nimbus behind his head,[3] and had it blessed at the tomb of the Apostle; then he chose a delicate rosary for Johanne, made from ivory and jet, carved with three tiny scallops on its central jet bead.[4] The combination offered threefold protection: the patronage of St James, prayers to the Virgin and jet to ward off the evil eye. He spent many hours walking in the streets of the city, talking to those members of his party who were staying for the festival, meeting English pilgrims who had come by boat to the coast of Spain and had walked in some cases for less than a week, or standing quietly on his own among the crowds of people in the cathedral nave, lost in his thoughts.

And then it was St James's Day. The long nave was packed for Mass, and all round it the squares were crowded too. The huge incense holder swung high and slow, sanctifying and fumigating the gathered pilgrims in one and the same action.[5] Bells, and a hundred candles on the altars around the great building where indulgences could be gained at every altar, on every day in this Holy Year, and reverent crowds, and strange muttered vernacular prayers swirling up with the clouds of incense all beat together on heaven's doors.

After Mass, when they had made their offerings, the pilgrims snaked slowly round the ambulatory, to see the majestic figure of the Apostle seated behind the high altar, and his tomb beneath it. They saw the sickle that had beheaded him, his chains, his walking staff, the head of St James the Less, a hair shirt of St Thomas Becket, and the remains of the red and white banner of St James that the Spanish Christians had carried into battle against the Moors.

But even then, Sutton's journey into Spain was not quite ended. First he must go to nearby Padrón, where St James's body was said to have first come ashore in a mysterious stone boat that might still be seen in the water. Then on farther, two days to the north-west, to Finisterre, the very extremity of the world, where 'one sees nothing anywhere but sky and water. They say that the water is so turbulent that no one can cross it and no one knows what lies beyond. It is said that some had tried to find out what was beyond and had sailed with galleys and ships … but only one galley returned and even on that galley most of the crew had died.'[6] Here at Finisterre, at the fingertips of the world, Sutton was confronted with his ultimate journey's end, the overwhelming power of forces beyond his control, in a place where mankind had only a toe-hold on the earth. A parable, if he still needed one, of pilgrimage and death.

Back in Compostela, there were other pilgrims arriving, other journeys ended and begun. For Sutton, it was the beginning of his homeward journey, a journey of reintegration, as July slipped into August and the earth turned brown. A journey into the remainder of his life, with new companions chosen from an abundance of grace. He would be recognized as a Compostela Pilgrim, his scallop on his hat. He would be given preferential lodging, reverential treatment, and his advice would be heeded.

As he travelled on, he relived his experiences as his journey unravelled back across the panorama of the road. His fears seemed smaller from the other side, the mountains easier to climb. In Castile, the corn was cut. In France the grapes were picked and pressed. In Normandy, the wolves lived on the wind. And when a mounted traveller chanced to meet him at Tewkesbury, he spurred his horse ahead to bring word of his coming. So as Sutton crossed the muddy Duck Brook in November, as the last leaves fell from the trees under a grey English sky, he raised his eyes and saw a great company of people coming out to meet him and bring him home. And when his journey was finally over, and they laid him to rest, he was remembered as he most wanted to be – as a pilgrim.

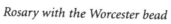

Rosary with the Worcester bead

Notes

Part I The Cockleshell Pilgrim
1 Tomb, Testament and Tower

1 Ezekiel 37.3.

2 *The Worcester Pilgrim* (Lubin, 1990).

3 Skeletal report by Wilkinson, in *The Worcester Pilgrim* (Lubin, 1990).

4 *A Calendar of Wills*, folios 3, 4 and 15 (ed. Fry, 1904). (Personal comment from Ms Jo Kirby.)

5 Pigment analysis carried out by the scientific department of the National Gallery.

6 *Anglo-Castilian Trade in the Later Middle Ages* (Childs, 1978).

7 Calculated from data in *Building in England Down to 1540* (Salzman, 1967).

8 'St Andrew's Church, Worcester' (Buchanan-Dunlop, 1937).

9 Found near Southwark Bridge on the Thames, Museum of London no. 250d. (Personal comment from Mr John Clarke.)

2 A Medieval Man

1 *William Langland's Piers Plowman* (circa 1380) (tr. Schmidt, 1992), p. 13.

2 *English Calendar of Fine Rolls*, vols 14 and 15 (HMSO).

3 *Collectanea* (Hamilton, 1912).

4 *Worcester Cathedral Muniments B class catalogue*, no. 1676.

5 *Piers Plowman* (tr. Schmidt, 1992), pp. 55–6.

6 *Piers Plowman* (tr. Schmidt, 1992), p. 78.

7 *Report of the Royal Commission on Historical Mss.*, 8.

8 *Ordnance Survey 1:500, first edition*, 1886.

9 *Ordinances of Worcester* (1467) (eds Smith and Smith, 1870).

10 The Feasts of the Purification (2 February), Annunciation (25 March), Visitation (2 July), Assumption (15 August), Nativity (8 September) and Conception (8 December) were all widely observed from the early Middle Ages.

11 *Worcester Cathedral Archives* Ms. C. 457.

12 *The Monastery and Cathedral of Worcester* (Noake, 1866), p. 116.

13 *The Obedientiary Account Rolls of Worcester* (Morrison, 1999).

Part II England
3 On the Road

1 *William Langland's Piers Plowman* (circa 1380) (tr. Schmidt, 1992), p. 65.

2 *A Parisian Journal*, entry for 1422 (tr. Shirley, 1968).

3 Now known as dysentery; it was common in hot weather in crowded conditions.

4 John Greene, Rector of St Andrew's Worcester 1421–4.

5 Matthew 5.28.

6 Ezekiel 18.2.

7 *The Book of Margery Kempe* (circa 1437) (ed. Meech, 1940), Book I, chapter 45, describing a pilgrimage of 1417.

8 From the Sarum Rite, order for blessing those going on a journey.

9 *English Gilds* (eds Smith and Smith, 1870); Lincoln 'Gild of the Resurrection', fifteenth century.

10 The base of one of the towers was recently discovered in a shop cellar.

11 *The Miracles of St James* (trs Coffey, Davidson and Dunn, 1996), from the twelfth-century Compostela pilgrim sermon 'Veneranda Dies'.

12 There were several medieval systems for measuring distances, varying regionally as well as between nations. The league was a common, but not a precisely fixed, unit throughout the period. Here it is standardized at 5 kilometres or 3 statute miles, roughly an hour's walk over moderate terrain.

13 *Ogilby's Britannia, 1675* (Facsimile edition, 1970).

14 *The Old Roads of Worcestershire* (Gwilliam, 1987). The site of this cross is reputed to be marked by the so-called 'cross tree' near the ford.

15 Sutton presumably had no idea it was a Roman road. It is now a footpath entering the village at the Old Rectory gate.

16 *John Leland's Itinerary* (circa 1545) (ed. Chandler, 1993), p. 193.

17 *John Leland's Itinerary* (ed. Chandler, 1993), p. 193.

18 Marsh Mallow, *Althaea officinalis*, grew freely in damp meadows and was used in various ways for a range of conditions from sore throats to raw skin.

4 By Severn to Bristol

1 *William Worcestre's Itineraries* (ed. Harvey, 1969). Reported by an old Bristol sailor, 1480.

2 *Historie of the Arrivall of Edward IV* (ed. Bruce, 1838). Written shortly after the decisive Battle of Tewkesbury, 1471.

3 *Public Works in Medieval Law* (ed. Flower, 1923), vol. 40.

4 Now the cathedral.

5 At first a toll booth and later a butter market, it still survives, but has been moved to Hillfield Gardens on the London Road.

6 *Bishop Morgan's Register*, 1422, ii, folio 8v. (Anon.).

7 *Ogilby's Britannia, 1675* (Facsimile edition, 1970).

8 *The Ancient and present state of Glostershire* (Atkyns, 1712).

9 Now the cathedral.

10 *William Worcestre's Itineraries* (ed. Harvey, 1969). As described in 1478.

11 *Treaty Rolls, 1428* (HMSO).

12 The English pilgrim William Wey counted 84 ships in the port of La Coruña in three days in 1456. Thirty-two of these vessels were English (Davey, 2000).

13 *Patent Rolls, May 9th, 1428* (HMSO).

14 *The Pilgrims Sea Voyage* (mid-fifteenth century) (ed. Furnivall, 1867).

5 Salisbury's Patient Saint

1 *John Leland's Itinerary* (circa 1545) (ed. Chandler, 1993), p. 499.

2 The original cross has been re-erected at Stourhead in Wiltshire.

3 *Italian Merchants* (Ruddock, 1951). 'Corinth raisins' were the best Greek currants.

4 'Hardyng's Chronicle' (1457) (ed. Kingsford, 1912).

5 *Trevisa's Polychronicon of Ranulphi Higden* (1387) (ed. Babington, 1865).

6 *John Leland's Itinerary* (ed. Chandler, 1993), pp. 406–7.

7 *Patent Rolls, July 11th, 1422* (HMSO).

8 *John Leland's Itinerary* (ed. Chandler, 1993), p. 405.

9 The George is still recognizably a fine medieval wayside inn.

10 'Aubrey's Natural History of Wiltshire, 1659'. Quoted in *The Bonhams* (Kidston, 1948).

11 *John Leland's Itinerary* (ed. Chandler, 1993), p. 493.

12 *S. Editha* (circa 1420) (ed. Horstmann, 1883).

13 Near the main entrance to Wilton House, built on the abbey site after the Dissolution.

14 Cited in 'The Miracles of St Osmund' (1424) (Brown, 1995).

15 Osmund was finally canonized in 1457.

16 No pope ever authenticated the Mottisfont Finger, which vanished without trace at the Reformation.

6 By Sea from Southampton

1 *The Libelle of Englyshe Polycye* (circa 1436) (ed. Warner, 1926).

2 *Papal Letters* (June 1410) (ed. Twemlow, 1904).

3 Still in use as a place of worship.

4 Huskard bought a licence in 1423, valid for 200 pilgrims, but the purchase of the ship was not completed until 15 July (Richmond, 1964; Storrs, 1998).

5 'The Trial of William Thorpe, 1407', as edited by William Tindale, 1530 (Pollard, 1903).

6 Black Book of Southampton 1. 98–9 (Platt, 1973).

7 *The Pilgrims Sea Voyage* (mid-fifteenth century) (ed. Furnivall, 1867).

8 *The Travels of Leo of Rozmital* (1465–7) (tr. Letts, 1957).

9 In 1120 the *White Ship* went down, taking with her Prince William, only son and heir of Henry I. There were almost no survivors.

10 *Chronique du Mont-Saint-Michel (1348–1468)* (ed. Luce, 1879).

11 *Dance of Death by Lydgate* (circa 1430), The Mayor's reply to Death (ed. Warren, 1931).

Part III Normandy
7 South from Cherbourg

1 Evidence from an elderly inhabitant of the district, early-fifteenth century (Quellien, 1983).

2 Attributed to the Marquis Albert Achille de Brandenbourg, who in 1449–50 caused the burning of 200 villages in southern Germany.

3 Ordinance of Charles VI of France, March 1388, concerning the roads around Paris.

4 *Trevisa's Polychronicon of Ranulphi Higden* (1387) (ed. Babington, 1865).

5 *A Parisian Journal*, entry for 1421 (tr. Shirley, 1968).

6 *Foedera*, 1422 (Rymer, 1709).

7 One of the medieval bridges on this road survives, at Pont Percé near Emondeville.

8 The Cross, and Our Lady of Coutances

1 John Lydgate (early-fifteenth century) (ed. MacCracken, 1911).

2 *Histoire religieuse* (Lerosey, undated).

3 The statue still survives, but the relic of the Cross was lost during the Revolution.

4 Christine de Pisan (early fifteenth century) (ed. Roy, 1886):
> 'You need not ask if they will curse / And brawl from drinking all that time;
>
> Each fracas makes a provost's fine: / All year he has a heavy purse!'

5 *Foedera*, 12 April 1418 (Rymer, 1709).

6 *Le Livre de Comptes de Thomas du Marest* (ed. Le Cacheux, 1905).

7 This statue is known from a ms. of circa 1100 (Forsyth, 1972).

8 The site is now the modern General Hospital.

9 *L'Hôtel-Dieu de Coutances* (Toussaint, 1967).

10 From a request for a papal indulgence, granted 1428 (Denifle, 1897, no. 214).

11 For the daily menus at a northern Maison-Dieu, see Delisle, 1859.

9 No Way to Mont St Michel

1 *Les Pèlerinages d'enfants* (1449) (Dupont, 1907): 'Dearly beloved Lord St Michael, what did you have in mind while you were building in the savage sea and on the Mount set in the sea? Lord have mercy.'

2 *Chronique du Mont-Saint-Michel* (1348–1468) (ed. Luce, 1879): '... nobody, of whatever rank or station, may go on pilgrimage to Mont St Michel, on pain of confiscation of goods and person. And anyone found to have done so in defiance of these proclamations and edicts is to be placed in the prisons of the said King our sovereign Lord ... '

3 *A Parisian Journal*, entry for 1413 (tr. Shirley, 1968).

4 A fourteenth-century fresco of two gossips in nearby Mésnil Aubert church neatly captures the mood.

5 *Holinshed's Chronicle, 1587* (ed. Wallace, 1923).

6 All these statues are still at La Lucerne.

7 *Chronique du Mont-Saint-Michel*, entry for 1420: 'La riviere de Caynon passa et courut lonc temps entre le Mont et Tombelaine' (ed. Luce, 1879).

8 Such a raid did eventually take place in late 1423, burning part of Genêts.

9 The story is first told in the twelfth-century 'Roman du Mont-Saint-Michel' by William de St Pair. The cross, last repaired in 1389, later vanished beneath the sands, but reappeared briefly in the early-seventeenth century (Beaurepaire, 1872).

10 'St Michael in Peril of the Sea'.

11 The skull is displayed in a magnificent reliquary in the church of St Gervais at Avranches.

10 Brigands or Bravehearts?

1 F. Villon, on receiving the death sentence (mid-fifteenth century):
> 'My name is François, so they say / Born near Paris out Pontoise way,
> And a length of rope some day / Will teach my neck what my buttocks weigh.'

2 From an appeal to the pope for financial aid, 1428 (Denifle, 1897, no. 200). The cathedral was not repaired for 50 years, fell into ruins again after the French Revolution and has now been demolished.

3 'Brigands, thieves, traitors and highwaymen'.

4 *La résistance* (Jouet, 1969); *Actes de La Chancellerie d'Henri VI* (Le Cacheux, 1907).

5 Von Harff used the old wooden bridge when he crossed the Sélune here in 1498 (tr. Letts, 1946).

6 So-called by the French, from the word that English soldiers used most often.

7 Although what it was, precisely, is not known.

8 The statue still stands in the St James parish church.

Part IV Brittany – Another Duchy
11 Independent Politics

1 From a sermon of San Bernardino (1380–1444).

2 Hebrews 13.2.

3 'Our Lady of the Blackbird's Nest'. Comprehensively wrecked in the French Revolution, the abbey is currently undergoing repair; many traces of its once extensive buildings survive nearby.

4 The hospital of St Yves is now the Tourist Information Office; the extant chapel is late fifteenth century.

5 Old Rennes was terribly prone to fires. Two conflagrations in 1456 and 1480 removed all trace of the city that Sutton saw, excepting only a few stone chapels. But much of the late medieval rebuilding still survives.

6 *The Pilgrimage of Arnold von Harff* (1496–9) (tr. Letts, 1946).

7 *A medieval handbook of travel* (Horstmann, 1888).

8 Many medieval churches had a 'Holy Ghost Hole' for this and other ceremonies.

9 A mark was worth 13s. 4d.

10 Prayer of St Vincent Ferrer (1350–1419).

12 Over the Loire

1 *The Pilgrimage of Arnold von Harff* (1496–9) (tr. Letts, 1946).

2 His name translates roughly as 'Gorge until you vomit'.

3 Gilles de Rais (1404–40) is better known to posterity as Bluebeard. His fortunes declined after the death of Joan of Arc, and he took to alchemy and satanic practices to try to restore them. Arrested in 1440, he was convicted of the murder of at least 200 infants and was put to death in Nantes.

4 A few years after this, Clisson finally tired of annual bills for repairing its wooden bridge, and the present stone one was built.

Part V Armagnac France
13 Through the Lands of Melusine

1 *Melusine, compiled 1382–1394* (ed. Donald, 1895).

2 From the Dedication to 'La Manière de Langue, May 1396', an English guide (with many errors!) to French (ed. Meyer, 1870).

3 *Histoire de Charles VII* (Vallet, 1862).

4 *Mandeville's Travels* (circa 1356). A largely fictitious account of his travels across the known world (ed. Seymour, 1968).

5 The 'Unicorn horns' known in the Middle Ages were in reality narwhal tusks. 'Dragon's Blood' was imported by Italians trading with Arab merchants who obtained it from the Island of Socotra off modern Yemen. It comes uniquely from the tree *Dracoena cinnabari*, and has had a wide range of uses through the ages, from a stain for marble, to fixing loose teeth (Alexander and Miller, 1996).

6 *Melusine* (ed. Donald, 1895).

7 *Melusine* (ed. Donald, 1895).

14 Marshes, Monks and Marauders

1 *Canterbury Tales* (circa 1386–1400), The Wife of Bath's Tale (ed. Skeat, 1894).

2 A total of 110 Franciscan houses were founded in France between 1350 and 1450, compared with just 12 in England.

3 'La Monastère des Cordeliers' (Garand, 1995).

4 The Antonines were skilled doctors, administering carefully controlled doses of what could be lethal mixtures.

5 'St Antony's fire' was mostly caused by ergot, a rare fungus that parasitizes cereals, especially rye. After a wet spring, rye bread made from contaminated flour spread the disease through entire communities, causing hallucinations, abortion, gangrene and death. Cattle turned into the stubble to graze often aborted or died as well, compounding the misery.

6 'Come Holy Ghost', sung in Latin or the vernacular at Pentecost services. The third verse had a particular resonance for a penitent pilgrim:
'Anoint and cheer our soiled face / With the abundance of thy grace: Keep far our foes, give peace at home; / Where thou art guide no ill can come.' (tr. Cosin).

7 The reforming mid-century bishop of Poitiers, Jacques Jouvenal, found on taking office that he had to arm his clergy with the 'Manuel des Curés' and order them to begin teaching their people the basics of Christian faith and practice; even the Ten Commandments were completely unknown to many.

8 Vix is now 25 kilometres inland. (From the Proceedings between the prior of Vix and the lieutenant of Fontenay.) A Royal Commission was set up in 1409 to restore the Marais Poitevin, but it achieved nothing and did not meet again until 1438. Drainage eventually recommenced in the seventeenth century (Clouzot, 1903).

9 Nearly 170 metres long and 22 metres wide, Les Halles was used until the Revolution.

10 The earliest known inn, La Petite Notre Dame, dates back to at least 1433 and is now the camera shop at 26 rue Porte-St-Jean. It retained its fifteenth-century façade statue of the Virgin and Child until 1929 (Clouzot and Farault, 1931).

15 The Holy Heads of St John

1 *Canterbury Tales* (circa 1386–1400), The Canon's Yeoman's Tale (ed. Skeat, 1894).

2 From the Accusation in a *Coquillards* trial at Dijon, October 1455 (Mackworth, 1947).

3 One Aragonese safe-conduct specifically permits a German party to enter the country in order to visit Compostela and see the Spanish way of life. The best descriptions of the curiosities encountered on pilgrimage are written by Germans, notably Leo of Rozmital (1465–7) and Arnold von Harff (1496–9).

4 For instance on 9 January 1409 Robert le Fourbisseur, canon of Laon in Picardy, was given leave, initially for seven weeks, to make a pilgrimage to Compostela. He was back at Laon by 17 May (Jacomet, 1996).

5 The *Pilgrim's Guide* (twelfth century) (tr. Hogarth, 1992). The actual complement of the abbey probably never exceeded 75 monks.

6 *Mandeville's Travels* (circa 1356) (ed. Seymour, 1968).

7 *Canterbury Tales*, The Prologue (ed. Skeat, 1894).

16 Troubled Times

1 From an appeal for a papal indulgence, 1429 (Denifle, 1897, no. 436).

2 The abbey suffered again in the sixteenth-century Wars of Religion, and all that remains today of the medieval building is a small section of one wall.

3 From an appeal for a papal indulgence, 1429 (Denifle, 1897, no. 436).

4 From an indulgence appeal, eventually granted in 1451 (Denifle, 1897, no. 438).

5 From an appeal for a papal indulgence, 1429 (Denifle, 1897, no. 439).

6 The stonemason's fees for shaping the stone shot are itemised in the town council accounts (eds d'Aussy and Saudau, 1902).

7 *The Pilgrimage of Arnold von Harff* (1496–9) (tr. Letts, 1946). The line of the old bridge and the causeway remains clearly visible, over marshy land that is still wet in early June. The chapel of the St James hospice is on private land, to the left of the road into the village.

8 From an appeal for a papal indulgence, 1420 (Denifle, 1897, no. 432).

9 From an appeal for a papal indulgence, 1427 (Denifle, 1897, no. 434).

10 Only the choir of Pleine Selve survives, but it makes a sizeable parish church. The valley still produces and markets its own wine.

Part VI Gascony
17 Ferry over the Gironde

1 *Trevisa's Polychronicon of Ranulphi Higden* (1387) (ed. Babington, 1865).

2 'St Martin's on the pilgrim road'.

3 *The Travels of Leo of Rozmital* (1465–7) (tr. Letts, 1957). The eleventh-century French epic 'Chanson de Roland' does not specify where the heroes Roland, Olivier and their companions were buried after the battle of Roncevaux, but the twelfth-century 'Pilgrim Guide' states 'His most blessed body was given respectful burial by his companions in the basilica of St Romain in Blaye' (tr. Hogarth, 1992).

4 *The Deeds of Don Pero Niño* (From an eyewitness account written in 1431–49) (tr. Evans, 1928).

18 Blessed Bordeaux

1 'Purchas' Pilgrim' (circa 1421–2) (Tate and Turville-Petre, 1995).

2 The founder was Duke William IX, Richard Coeur de Lion's great-grandfather.

3 From the foundation charter, AD 1119.

4 Ascribed to Pope Innocent VI and used as a prayer by medieval congregations:
'Hail to thee! True Body sprung / From the Virgin Mary's womb!
The same that on the cross was hung, / And bore for man the bitter doom.
Thou whose side was pierced and flowed / Both with water and with blood,
Suffer us to taste of thee, / In our life's last agony.' (Trad.) .

5 Thomas Aquinas, from the Mass for Corpus Christi: 'Behold, the Bread of Angels, Sent to pilgrims in their banishment ...' (Trad.).

6 Verse 6 of 'Sacris Solemnis' by Thomas Aquinas, sung at Corpus Christi:
'Bread of the angel hosts, here mankind's bread is made;
Heaven's bread now casts earths dreams in its shade;
O what a glorious feat! Even the humblest slave
Poorest, lowliest, of their Lord eat.'

7 The remains of a Roman temple, which survived until the seventeenth century.

8 *The Pilgrimage of Arnold von Harff* (1496–9) (tr. Letts, 1946). All that remains of the shrine is a green sarcophagus beneath the high altar.

9 From a description of St Seurin's church, 1445 (Denifle, 1897, no. 351).

10 'St Fort' was another spurious saint, his name being a corruption of 'Strength'.

11 From an appeal to the pope, 1419 (Denifle, 1897, no. 350).

12 In 1408 an Easter mystery play was staged outside the Carmelite convent, a few blocks away from the Hospital of St James (Ribadieu, 1884).

13 Now in the Museum of Aquitaine, Bordeaux.

14 Shortly thereafter, St Julian's was demolished by an invading French army and in 1446 an appeal was made for its reconstruction (Denifle, 1897, no. 354).

15 As described in 1426 (Denifle, 1897, no. 350). The cross still stands in the St Geniès district of southern Bordeaux.

16 The Bardanac house was one of the first to suffer as the French armies closed in. By 1426 it wanted 'extensive repairs in its buildings and properties ... it is feared the hospital will be completely ruined' (Denifle, 1897, no. 355).

19 The Road through the Landes

1 Andrew Borde on his return to Gascony (circa 1540) (ed. Furnivall, 1870).

2 Sutton's journey through the Landes was at the late peak of its prosperity and fertility. Most of this medieval landscape is now lost, buried up to 12 metres deep in the sands that blew in from the coast in the seventeenth and eighteenth centuries and hidden under the pine forest that was subsequently planted on top (*Mimizan*, Anon., undated).

3 About a dozen such houses in one segment of the Landes are named repeatedly in a series of medieval wills of the ruling Albret family.

4 The Le Barp crosses are long since gone, but several of the nine stone pyramids, once over two metres tall and topped with iron crosses, that delimited the boundaries of Mimizan Priory can still be seen in situ.

5 *The Pilgrimage of Arnold von Harff* (1496–9) (tr. Letts, 1946).

6 Thanks to continuing generous donations, Poymartet flourished into at least the sixteenth century. But by a survey of 1827, all that remained were a few ancient vines (Louty, 1995).

Part VII Navarre
20 Echoes of Roland

1 *Froissart's Chronicles*, entry for 1367 (tr. Jolliffe, 1967).

2 *Pèlerins de Saint-Jacques* (Urrutibéhéty, 1993).

3 A New Hospital document of 1411 indicates it then had seven brothers on the staff, all natives of Arancou, ranging in age from 55 to 88 (Urrutibéhéty, 1993).

4 It had 60 hearths compared to 55 in Garris in the mid-fourteenth century.

5 The ditches ran along the line of the present rue Gambetta. After a threatened uprising in 1398, the decision was taken to flood the hitherto dry ditches and form a moat, a task that was eventually carried out by a Breton engineer in 1438.

6 From a grant of Jean II of Navarre in 1472, to maintain its ancient obligations, 'so the poor pilgrims in this hospital can be made at home and cared for'.

7 In the fourteenth-century tax assessment, Ostabat had 69 hearths; St Palais had 60; and St-Jean-Pied-de-Port had 63. Henri IV in the sixteenth century called it 'the main commercial town and staging post in our Kingdom of (Lower) Navarre'. Now dwarfed by its neighbours, it is a shrunken husk of its former self, lying quietly with its memories, off the main road.

8 The so-called 'Donati Christo', those who had given themselves to Christ.

9 Harambeltz, one of the smallest but best documented donat priories, consisted of a chapel and hospital of St Nicholas and four donat houses, which are still owned by the descendants of the original four families.

10 *The Pilgrimage of Arnold von Harff* (1496–9) (tr. Letts, 1946).

11 'Purchas' Pilgrim' (circa 1421–2) (Tate and Turville-Petre, 1995).

12 The Campana de la Valcarlos is mentioned in 1428. Nompar, Lord of Caumont stayed in the Capeyron Rouge in 1417.

13 'Purchas' Pilgrim' (Tate and Turville-Petre, 1995).

14 'Vous qui allez à St Iacques / Je vous prie humblement
Que n'ayez point de haste: / Allez tout bellement.
Las! que les pauvres malades / Sont en grand desconfort!
Car maints hommes et femmes / Par les chemins sont morts.'
(Anonymous French)

21 Islam and Jewry

1 From 'La Preciosa', a twelfth-century poem in honour of Roncevaux.

2 Data from the abbey's accounts (Garcia, undated).

3 On 8 September 1423, a proclamation ordered that the three districts of Pamplona be united into one city.

4 In the 1494 tax returns, there were 74 Jewish households in the Pamplona ghetto, of which 58 were wealthy enough to pay tax. Jews made up about 3.5 per cent of the population of Navarre throughout the fifteenth century (Gampel, 1989).

5 Andrew Borde's epitome of Navarre, circa 1540 (ed. Furnivall, 1870).

6 In exchange, England imported Navarrese licorice, almonds, sailcloth, fine cordwain and basan (Childs, 1978).

7 The population of Navarre at this time was about 100,000.

8 *Hermann Künig von Vach* (1495) (tr. Durant, 1993).

9 General safe-conduct of Jean II, for the Holy Year 1434.

10 *The Pilgrimage of Arnold von Harff* (1496–9) (tr. Letts, 1946).

11 Now in the Church of the Crucifix, Puenta La Reina.

22 The War-torn Border

1 'Purchas' Pilgrim' (circa 1421–2) (Tate and Turville-Petre, 1995). Gruon is probably Logroño. Lines 55 to 68, covering the section from Pamplona to Santo Domingo, appear to be reversed in the manuscript. This may be because it was written on the basis of advice from a returning pilgrim, or because the poem was composed later, with reference to a text describing the eastward journey.

2 Now displayed in the church of San Miguel.

3 *Famines et épidémis* (Berthe, 1984).

4 Data from Navarrese account books. A carapito measure was about 12 litres (Hamilton, 1936).

5 The twelfth-century bridge was used until 1884, when the present one was built on the same site.

6 'Purchas' Pilgrim' (Tate and Turville-Petre, 1995).

Part VIII Camino across Castile
23 The Way of St James

1 'Purchas' Pilgrim' (circa 1421–2) (Tate and Turville-Petre, 1995).

2 Nompar de Caumont (1417) (Massie, 1992). This is the earliest detailed account of the miracle. The girl later confessed to her crime, and was herself hanged. Similar events are recorded in England, usually resulting in a royal pardon because of the 'miracle'. In 1363, for instance, Walter Wynkeburne of Leicester revived on his way to the cemetery and was given sanctuary so he could not be returned to the gallows (Lumby, 1895).

3 *The Travels of Leo of Rozmital* (1465–7) (tr. Letts, 1957).

4 *Hermann Künig von Vach* (1495) (tr. Durant, 1993). This tale of pilgrim-poisoning is also known from a medieval German song.

5 Now deconsecrated, the church serves as the town's public library.

6 After several false starts, León and Castile were united under Ferdinand III (1230–52).

7 'Nuestra Señora La Blanca' has been moved inside the cathedral for protection from the elements, and a modern copy substituted. Both pillars show wear from the hands of generations of grateful pilgrims.

8 'A singing pilgrim scares away many thieves.'

9 *The Book of Margery Kempe* (referring to a pilgrimage to Aachen in 1433) (ed. Meech, 1940) Book II, chapter 6.

10 Nompar, Lord of Caumont-sur-Garonne, left his castle on 8 July 1417 and returned on 3 September, after a pilgrimage to Compostela and Finisterre (Massie, 1992).

11 *The Pilgrimage of Arnold von Harff* (1496–9) (tr. Letts, 1946).

12 Hinrich Dunkelgud, a rising young grocer of Lübeck, described his pilgrimage of 1479 in these terms in his trade notebooks (ed. Mantels, 1881).

13 The Somport pass over the central Pyrenees was less favoured by fifteenth-century pilgrims, who tended instead to use the more westerly Roncevaux route.

14 Chaucer's fictional Wife of Bath was probably based on a type quite commonly found on the pilgrim roads. Not as outspokenly religious as Margery Kempe, they were nevertheless sincerely pious and had few other outlets for their spiritual hunger. Kempe mentions, for instance, meeting one Margaret Florentyne, 'comyn fro Rome [to Assisi] to purchasyn hir pardon' (Book I, chapter 31) (ed. Meech, 1940).

15 Vielliard (1936) cites an Aragonese safe-conduct issued in 1415 in Catalan for one Jacobus Brente, who since 'he does not know the language of the peoples of our said realms and territories and is black and of the colour of the Ethiopians [conventionally equated with a devil], one fears that some injustice or harm be done to him'.

16 Verses 1 and 2 of the traditional pilgrim song 'Dum Paterfamilias':
'God, Father of all mankind, King, ruler of all the world
Gave to his Apostles dear, lands, each to their own just care
James, in his own land of Spain, Shines out with a holy flame.
*First among Apostles now! Martyred at Jerusalem!
James become the holiest by illustrious martyrdom!

Lo! James's Galicia calls out for our pious toil,
Marching on the holy way, road over her glorious soil.
Blending all our prayers in one harmony of endless song:
To Lord St James! To God's St James!
And Onward! And Upward! God, speed our way.'

24 Mountains and Miracles

1 *Hermann Künig von Vach* (1495) (tr. Durant, 1993).

2 'Purchas' Pilgrim' (circa 1421–2) (Tate and Turville-Petre, 1995).

3 *Hermann Künig von Vach* (tr. Durant, 1993).

4 The church was rebuilt in the sixteenth century.

5 The Spanish pope Callistus III (1455–8) formalized the tradition of appealing to the 'Door of Pardon' and decreed that pilgrims who were genuinely unable to fullfil their vows could thenceforward obtain their full indulgence at Santiago's church in Villafranca.

6 From the foundation charter, 1375.

7 The Ribadiso hospital has recently been restored as a pilgrim refuge.

25 Journey's End

1 'Purchas' Pilgrim' (circa 1421–2) (Tate and Turville-Petre, 1995).

2 This form of words, known since the fourteenth century, is essentially the same as that used in the 'compostela' given to modern pilgrims.

3 This unusual motif appears in the set of roof bosses Robert Sutton paid for in Worcester, and on a fifteenth-century pilgrim badge recovered from the Thames in London (See Chapter 1, note 9).

4 Compostela and Whitby, in Yorkshire, were the only sources of quality medieval jet work. A single jet bead of this type was found in an undated late medieval deposit in the Deansway excavations in Worcester (Dalwood and Edwards, 2001).

5 The first record of a giant censer at Compostela is in the fourteenth century. The present 'Botafumeiro' was made to replace one lost during the Napoleonic Wars.

6 *The Travels of Leo of Rozmital* (1465–7) (tr. Letts, 1957).

References

Alexander, D. and Miller, A. (1996), 'Saving the spectacular flora of Socotra', *Plant Talk* 7, pp. 19–22.

Anon. (undated), *Mimizan des origines à 1900*. Centre d'essais des Landes, Biscarrosse.

Anon. (unpublished) 'The Registers of Bishop Morgan'. Worcester County Record Office.

Atkyns, Sir Robert (1712), *The Ancient and present state of Glostershire*.

Babington, C. (ed.) (1865), *Polychronicon of Ranulphi Higden, monachi Cestrensis, together with English translations of John Trevisa and of an unknown writer of the fifteenth century*. Rolls Series 41, London.

Beaurepaire, E. de Robillard de (ed.) (1872), *Histoire Générale de l'Abbaye du Mont-St-Michel au Peril de la Mer. Par Dom Jean Huynes (1639)*. Librarie de la Société de l'Histoire de Normandie 1, A. Le Brument, Rouen.

Berthe, M. (1984), *Famines et épidémies dans les campagnes navarraises à la fin du moyen age. 2 tomes*. SFIED, Paris.

Brown, A. D. (1995), *Popular Piety in Late Medieval England. The Diocese of Salisbury 1250–1550*. Clarendon Press, Oxford.

Bruce, J. (ed.) (1838), *Historie of the Arrivall of Edward IV in England and the finall recoverye of his kingdomes from Henry VI. AD 1471*. Camden Society, 1.

Buchanan-Dunlop, W. R. (1937), 'St Andrew's Church, Worcester', *Transactions of the Worcester Archaeological Society* 14, pp. 18–29.

Carus-Wilson, E. M. (ed.) (1967), *The Overseas Trade of Bristol in the Late Middle Ages*. Merlin Press, London.

Chandler, J. (ed.) (1993), *John Leland's Itinerary: Travels in Tudor England*. Sutton Publishing, Stroud.

Childs, W. R. (1978), *Anglo-Castilian Trade in the later Middle Ages*. Manchester University Press.

Clouzot, E. (1903), *Les Marais de la Sèvre Niortaise et du Lay du Xe à la fin du XVIe siècle*. Bulletin et Mémoires de la Société des Antiquaires de l'Ouest, 2ième série 27, Poitiers.

Clouzot, H. and Farault, A. (1931), *Niort et sa banlieue. Dictionnaire Topographique et historique, avec plan du XIeme au XVIIIeme siècle*. Société historique et scientifique des Deux-Sèvres, Niort.

Coffey, T. F., Davidson, L. K. and Dunn, M. (trs and eds) (1996), *The Miracles of St James*. Italica Press, New York.

Dalwood, H. and Edwards, R. (2001), *The Deansway Excavations, Draft Publication Report*. Worcestershire Archaeological Service.

d'Aussy, D. and Saudau, M. L.-C. (eds) (1902), *Registres de l'échevinage de Saint-Jean d'Angély, tome 3*. Archives historiques de La Saintonge et de l'Aunis 32.

Davey, F. (2000), *William Wey: An English Pilgrim to Compostella in 1456*. Confraternity of St James, London.

Delisle, L. V. (1859), *Fragments de l'Histoire de Gonesse*. Paris.

Denifle, H. (1897), *La Désolation des Eglises, Monastères et Hôpitaux en France Pendant la Guerre de Cent Ans, tome 2*. Paris.

Donald, A. K. (tr. and ed.) (1895), *Melusine, compiled (1382–94 AD) by Jean d'Arras. Englisht about 1500*. Early English Text Society extra series 68.

Dupont, E. (1907), *Les Pèlerinages d'enfants allemands au Mont-Saint-Michel (XVeme siècle)*. Librarie Historique des Provinces, Paris.

Durant, J. (tr. and ed.) (1993), *Hermann Künig von Vach. The Pilgrim and Path to St James*. Confraternity of St James Occasional Paper 3, London.

Evans, J. (tr.) (1928), *The Unconquered Knight. A Chronicle of the Deeds of Don Pero Niño Count of Buelna by his standard-bearer Gutierre Diaz de Gamez (1431–1449)*. Routledge and Sons, London.

Flower, C. T. (1915, 1923), *Public Works in Medieval Law, 2 volumes*. Selden Society, London, 32 and 40.

Forsyth, I. H. (1972), *The Throne of Wisdom: wood sculptures of the Madonna in Romanesque France*. Princeton University Press.

Fry, A. E. (ed.) (1904), *A Calendar of Wills and Administrations preserved in the consistory court of the bishop of Worcester, volume I: 1451–1600*. Worcester Historical Society; also published as volume 31 of The Index Library, British Record Society, London.

Furnivall, F. J. (ed.) (1867), *The Pilgrims Sea Voyage. From the Trinity College Cambridge Ms. R. 3, 19, t. Hen VI*. Early English Text Society 25.

Furnivall, F. J. (ed.) (1870), *The Fyrst Boke of the Introduction of Knowledge and other works of Andrew Borde, Doctor of Physick*. Early English Text Society extra series 10.

Gampel, B. R. (1989), *The Last Jews on Iberian Soil: Navarrese Jewry 1479–1498*. University of California Press, Berkeley.

Garand, R. (1995), 'La Monastère des Cordeliers de Bressuire', *Revue d'Histoire du Pays Bressuirais* 44, pp. 50–7.

Garcia, R. Jebús (undated), 'The Racionero accounts of Roncesvalles Abbey (in Spanish)', *Compostela* First series 17, pp. 4–9, Santiago de Compostela.

Gwilliam, H. W. (1987), *The Old Roads of Worcestershire*. Author's typescript, deposited at Worcester History Centre.

Hamilton, E. J. (1936), *Money, Prices and Wages in Valencia, Aragon and Navarre, 1351–1500*. Harvard Economic Studies 51, Harvard University Press.

Hamilton, S. G. (1912), *Collectanea. (Being a translation of charters etc. found in a thirteenth century chest in St Swithin's.)* Worcester Historical Society.

Harvey, J. H. (ed.) (1969), *William Worcestre's Itineraries. Edited from the unique Ms. Corpus Christi College Cambridge, 210*. Clarendon Press, Oxford.

HMSO, Calendar of Patent Rolls, Calendar of Treaty Rolls, English Calendar of Fine Rolls.

Hogarth, J. (tr.) (1992), *The Pilgrim's Guide. A 12th Century Guide for the Pilgrim to St James of Compostella*. Confraternity of St James, London.

Horstmann, C. (ed.) (1883), *S. Editha sive Chronicon Vilodunense im Wiltshire Dialeckt. Aus ms. Cotton Faustina B III*. Heilbronn.

Horstmann, C. (ed.) (1888), *A medieval handbook of travel*. Englische Studien 8.

Jacomet, H. (1996), 'Pierre Plumé, Gilles Mureau, Jehan Piedefer, chanoines de Chartres. Pèlerins de Terre Sainte et de Galice 1483–4 et 1517–18', *Bulletin de la Société Archéologique d'Eure et Loire* 48 (pp. 1–32), 49, 50 and supplement.

Jolliffe, J. (tr. and ed.) (1967), *Froissart's Chronicles*. Harville Press, London.

Jouet, R. (1969), *La résistance à l'occupation anglaise en Basse-Normandie, 1418–1450*. Cahier des Annales de Normandie 5.

Kidston, G. J. (1948), *The Bonhams of Wiltshire and Essex*. C. H. Woodward, Devizes.

Kingsford, C. L. (ed.) (1912), 'Extracts from the first version of Hardyng's Chronicle', *English Historical Review* 27 pp. 744–5 and 749.

Le Cacheux, P. (ed.) (1905), *Le Livre de Comptes de Thomas du Marest, curé de St-Nicholas de Coutances (1397–1433), suivi de pièces du 15ème siècle relatives au Diocèse et au Evêques de Coutances*. Société de l'Histoire de Normandie, Rouen and Paris.

Le Cacheux, P. (1907), *Actes de La Chancellerie d'Henri VI concernant La Normandie sous La Domination Anglaise (1422–1435), 2 tomes*. Société de l'Histoire de Normandie, Rouen and Paris.

Lerosey, A. (undated), *Histoire religieuse et civile de Périers et ses notabilités*. Paris.

Letts, M. (tr.) (1946), *The Pilgrimage of Arnold von Harff*. Hakluyt Society, London, second series 94.

Letts, M. (tr.) (1957), *The Travels of Leo of Rozmital*. Hakluyt Society, London, second series 108.

Louty, J. C. (1995), 'Prieuré-Hôpital de Poymartet (Landes)', *Bourdon*. Amis de St-Jacques de Compostelle en Aquitaine, Gradignan, n. s. 8.

Lubin, H. (1990), *The Worcester Pilgrim*. Worcester Cathedral Publications 1.

Luce, S. (ed.) (1879), *Chronique du Mont-Saint-Michel (1348–1468). Publiée avec notes et pièces diverses relatives au Mont-Saint-Michel et à la défense nationale en basse normandie pendant l'Occupation Anglaise. 2 tomes*. Société des Anciens Textes Françaises.

Lumby, J. R. (ed.) (1895), *Knighton's Chronicle part II*. Rolls Series.

MacCracken, H. N. (ed.) (1911), *The Minor Poems of John Lydgate, Part I: Religious Poems*. Early English Text Society 192.

Mackworth, C. (1947), *François Villon: a study with an introduction by Denis Saurat*. Westhouse, London.

Mantels, W. (1881), 'Aus dem Memorial-oder Geheim Buche des Lübecker Krämers Hinrich Dunkelgud', chapter 9 of Mantels, W. (ed.), *Beiträge zur lübisch-hansischen Geschichte*. Jena.

Massie, J. (1992), 'La route du Seigneur de Caumont', *Bourdon*. Amis de St-Jacques de Compostelle en Aquitaine, Gradignan, n. s. 2 p. 49, and 3.

Meech, S. B. (ed.) (1940), *The Book of Margery Kempe*. Early English Text Society, 212.

Meyer, P. (ed.) (1870), 'La Manière de Langue', *Revue Critique* 10, p. 373.

Morrison, D. J. (1999), *The Obedientiary Account Rolls of Worcester Cathedral Priory 1469–1540*. Unpublished PhD Thesis, Birmingham University.

Noake, J. (1866), *The Monastery and Cathedral of Worcester*. London.

Ogilby, J. (1675), *Britannia*. Published in facsimile in 1970 by Theatrum Orbis Terrarum Ltd, Amsterdam.

Platt, C. (1973), *Medieval Southampton. The port and trading community, AD 1000–1600*. Routledge and Kegan Paul, London and Boston.

Pollard, A. W. (ed.) (1903), *Fifteenth Century Prose and Verse*. Constable.

Quellien, J. (1983), *Histoire des Populations du Cotentin*. Brionne.

Ribadieu, H. (1884), *La Guyenne d'Autrefois. Ses clercs, ses abbés, ses moines, ses églises et ses monastères*. Féret et fils, Bordeaux.

Richmond, C. F. (1964), 'The Keeping of the seas during the Hundred Years War: 1422–1440', *History* 49, pp. 283–98.

Roy, M. (ed.) (1886), *Christine de Pisan: Le Livre de la mutacion de fortune, III*. La Société des Anciens Textes Françaises.

Ruddock, A. A. (1951), *Italian Merchants and shipping in Southampton. 1270–1600*. Southampton University College Press.

Rymer, T. (1709), *Foedera, volumes 9 and 10*. A. and J. Churchill, London.

Salzman, L. F. (1967), *Building in England down to 1540. A documentary history*. Oxford University Press, second edition.

Schmidt, A. V. C. (tr.) (1992), *William Langland's Piers Plowman*. Oxford University Press.

Seymour, M. C. (ed.) (1968), *Mandeville's Travels*. Oxford University Press.

Shirley, J. (tr. and ed.) (1968), *A Parisian Journal 1405–1449. Translated from the anonymous Journal d'un Bourgeois de Paris.* Clarendon Press, Oxford.

Skeat, W. (ed.) (1894), *The Complete Works of Geoffrey Chaucer: Canterbury Tales (Text).* Clarendon Press, Oxford.

Smith, T. and Smith, L. T. (eds) (1870), *English Gilds. The Original Ordinances of more than one hundred Early English Gilds; together with Ye Olde Usages of Ye cite of Wynchestre; the Ordinances of Worcester; the Office of the Mayor of Bristol; and the Costomary of the Manor of Tettenhall-Regis. From original manuscripts of the fourteenth and fifteenth centuries.* Early English Text Society 40.

Storrs, C. M. (1998), *Jacobean Pilgrims from England to St James of Compostella from the early twelfth to the late fifteenth century.* Confraternity of St James, London.

Tate, R. B. and Turville-Petre, T. (1995), *Two pilgrim itineraries of the later Middle Ages.* Xunta de Galicia, Compostela.

Toussaint, J. (1967), *L'Hôtel-Dieu de Coutances. Les Augustines et l'Hôpital Général. Huit siècles d'histoire régionale.* Editions OCEP, Coutances.

Twemlow, J. A. (ed.) (1904), *Calendar of entries in the papal registers relating to Great Britain and Ireland. Papal Letters vols 6 and 7.* HMSO, London.

Urrutibéhéty, C. (1993), *Pèlerins de Saint-Jacques. La Traversée du Pays Basque.* Editions J et D, Biarritz.

Vallet, M. A. (1862), *Histoire de Charles VII, Roi de France, et de son époque. 1403–1461. 3 tomes.* Paris.

Vielliard, J. (1936), 'Pèlerins d'Espagne à la fin du moyen âge. Ce que nous apprennent les sauf-conduits délivrés aux pèlerins par la chancellerie des rois d'Aragon entre 1379 et 1422', *Analecta Sacra Tarraconensia* 12, pp. 265–300.

Wallace, R. S. (ed.) (1923), *Holinshed's Chronicles, 1587.* Oxford University Press.

Warner, G. (ed.) (1926), *The Libelle of Englyshe Polycye.* Clarendon Press, Oxford.

Warren, F. (ed.) (1931), *The Dance of Death by Lydgate.* Early English Text Society 181.

Further Reading

1 Background to the period

Armstrong, C. A. J. (1983), *England, France and Burgundy in the Fifteenth Century.* Hambledon Press, London.

Duffy, E. (1992), *The Stripping of the Altars: Traditional religion in England 1400–1580.* Yale University Press, New York and London.

Nilson, B. (1998), *Cathedral Shrines of Medieval England.* Boydell Press, Suffolk.

2 Guides for modern pilgrims

The Confraternity of Saint James in London (www.csj.org.uk) publishes a regularly updated series of English-language practical guides to the Spanish camino and some of the French routes leading to it. Similar guides are published by other European associations.

There are innumerable more bulky guides to the pilgrimage. Two good ones are:

Lozano, M. B., *A Practical Guide for Pilgrims.* Editorial Everest. Available in several languages and editions.

Valiña, E. S. (1992 currently out of print), *The Pilgrim's Guide to the Camino de Santiago, translated into English by Laurie Dennett.* Galaxia.

Glossary

Antonines The Order of Hospital Brothers of St Antony, who cared especially for victims of 'St Antony's Fire'. They wore black robes and a blue T-shaped cross, and carried bells that they rang as they rode round seeking alms for their hospitals.

Armagnacs The main French faction loyal to the Dauphin, later Charles VII of France. Also called the Orleanists, they were named after their most prominent leaders. By the 1420s, they were fighting against the English.

assart A clearing in a forest, used as arable land.

Augustinians The Order of Black Canons, or the Canons Regular. They lived in monasteries but typically involved themselves with the surrounding communities, teaching, running hospitals, etc.

balinger A small ship lacking a forecastle, used for coastal and cross-Channel trade.

basan Tanned sheepskins.

Bedford Duke John of Bedford, Henry V's most talented brother, who acted as Regent in France for his nephew the infant Henry VI.

Benedictines The spiritual parent of most Orders of enclosed monks, they wore a black habit and based their Rule on the works of St Benedict of Nursia (died circa 550).

Brittany An independant Duchy, owing homage to the Crown of France, but closely linked to England by treaty obligations.

Burgundians The main French faction opposed to the Dauphin; followers of the Dukes of Burgundy, a branch of the royal family with vast lands in eastern France. In the 1420s they were closely allied to the English.

burnet A dark-brown fine cloth.

camino The Spanish term for the Way of St James.

canon A member of a religious community following a rule which required more 'stability' than the mendicant friars but more flexibility to mix with the outside world than the true monastics.

Carmelites The Order of Our Lady of Mount Carmel, or Whitefriars. They wore a brown habit, black scapula and white mantle, and were primarily concerned with asceticism and contemplation.

carrack A large merchant vessel, usually armed.

Carthusians A strictly contemplative Order. The monks were vowed to silence and lived alone except for church services, the manual work being done by lay brothers.

Cistercians The White Monks, who aimed to return to primitive Benedictine purity, founding their greatest Houses in remote places; they soon became wealthy through successful farming, and became less rigorous.

cordwain Fine grained leather, from goats or sometimes horses, used in the luxury shoe-making trade. Originally exclusively from Córdoba in southern Spain, it later became more widespread. In England, cordwainers had a monopoly on making new shoes; cobblers were only permitted to mend them and to sell reconditioned footwear.

Dauphin Title of the heir to the Crown of France.

Dominicans The Order of Preaching Friars (OP), or Blackfriars, who had a special responsibility for education. In France they are known as Jacobins because their first house there was dedicated to St James.

double monastery One with both monks and nuns, segregated for most of their time but usually sharing a church for worship.

Franciscans The Order of Friars Minor (OFM), or Greyfriars, who had a special devotion to poverty and care of the poor.

friars Members of a mendicant or begging Order (e.g. the Franciscans), who were not confined to their convents but travelled round working and begging for food. By the fifteenth century, many had lapsed from their founders' ideals of poverty.

galley   A single-decked ship with a sail and oars, favoured by the Mediterranean merchants.

Hospitallers   A knightly Order, founded in the late-eleventh century and based initially in Jerusalem at the Hospital of St John the Baptist. From 1310 they were based in Rhodes, and after 1530 they moved again and became known as the Knights of Malta. They protected pilgrims and ran hospitals, and took over most of the Templar lands in France. Their uniform was a black cloak and a white eight-pointed Maltese Cross.

Hôtel-Dieu   An institution devoted to the care of pilgrims and the sick, with a resident staff living under a religious Rule.

indulgence   The remission by the Church of the temporal penalty due for sins, after those sins have been forgiven. The concept depended on the notion that a sin necessarily led to punishment, either on earth or, in later thought, in Purgatory. This punishment could be cancelled by the reservoir of 'merit' accumulated by Christ and the saints, either by a particular papal decree or by the prayers and pious actions of the living faithful.

Lancastrians   The dynasty (and its supporters) set up by Henry IV of England when he overthrew his cousin Richard II.

madder   A reddish-purple dye obtained from the root of *Rubia tinctorum*, also grown for medicinal purposes.

Maison-Dieu   See Hôtel-Dieu.

murrey   Dark purple-red cloth.

plenary   An indulgence that covered all punishment due for sins committed and forgiven.

Premonstratensians   An austere Order of canons who abstained from all meat. Also known as the White Canons.

relic Any portion of the body of a saint, including the Body of Christ, or anything that had come into contact with such an item, which was the focus for a cult of veneration. Many were displayed in costly reliquaries.

Sack Friars A small Order of Mendicants, also known as the Friars of the Penance of Jesus Christ. They were ordered to cease admitting new brothers in 1274, and many houses amalgamated with those of other Orders.

scaffa A small undecked vessel, often used as a fishing boat.

Seigneur French term for 'Lord', used for 'lord of the manor', 'saint' and, occasionally, God.

Templars A knightly Order, founded in 1118 to defend Jerusalem and protect pilgrims to the Holy Land. They became very wealthy, fell foul of the King of France, and were forcibly disbanded in 1312.

Trinitarian Friars The Order of the Most Holy Trinity, or the Mathurins. They wore white habits with a bicoloured cross (red upright and blue crossbar) on the scapula, and devoted themselves to ransoming Christian captives and running hospitals for pilgrims.

Troyes The Treaty of 1420, hailed at the time as the Final Peace between England and France, and the end to the wars. It proved to be nothing of the kind. Under it, Henry V of England became heir to the throne of France, and Regent for his father-in-law the ailing French King Charles VI. When both Henry and Charles died within a few months of each other in 1422, the infant Henry VI was proclaimed King of both England and France.

tun A measure of volume (and hence of the capacity of ships), equivalent to a standard wine barrel.

Victorines A prestigious French branch of the Augustinian canons, especially dedicated to study and mysticism.

Made in the USA
Lexington, KY
24 November 2013